The PRAISE AND WORSHIP TEAM instant Tune-up

The PRAISE and WORSHIP Team instant Tune-up

Doug and Tami Flather

ZONDERVAN™

GRAND RAPIDS, MICHIGAN 49530

ZONDERVAN™

The Praise and Worship Team Instant Tune-Up
Copyright © 2002 by Douglas Flather and Tami Flather

Requests for information should be addressed to:

Zondervan, *Grand Rapids, Michigan 49530*

Library of Congress Cataloging-in-Publication Data
Flather, Douglas R., 1960-
     The praise and worship team instant tune-up! / Doug and Tami Flather.
        p. cm.
     Includes bibliographical references.
     ISBN 0-310-24232-0
     1. Contemporary Christian music—Instruction and study.   2. Church music—
Instruction and study.   I. Flather, Tami, 1964-   II. Title.
MT88 .F53 2002
781.71'043—dc21
                           2001005287

Interior design by Todd Sprague

Printed in the United States of America

02 03 04 05 06 07 08 / ❖ ML/ 10 9 8 7 6 5 4 3

Contents

10.39

1047|7

Special Thanks

We've learned from many, many gifted artists and leaders over the years, but we want to thank three special people who helped make this resource possible.

Audrey Hunt of the Audrey Hunt Vocal Company is a professional vocal coach from California who specializes in distance-learning vocalist resources, including her award-winning Anyone Can Sing! program. Audrey both reviewed and contributed to chapter 3. We recommend you look into her resources at www.singtome.com.

Gary Young, one of the instrumental directors at Cedar Ridge Community Church, reviewed the chapter for players and offered some great suggestions.

Larry Compter reviewed the entire manuscript and offered editorial insights that greatly enhanced our work. He's a great friend and terrific worship team member.

Doug and Tami Flather can be reached via email at worshiptuneup@juno.com

intRoDuCtion

During the days of the Old Testament, one of the ways people worshiped was through animal sacrifice. As you probably know, God's people were admonished to offer the very best of their flock. Animals that were injured, blemished, or otherwise less than their best were prohibited.

In the New Testament, believers are encouraged to "continually offer to God a sacrifice of praise" (Hebrews 13:15).

It is not overextending the metaphor to suggest that God continues to desire our contemporary vocal and instrumental "sacrifices" be characterized by the same spirit of bringing our best to the altar.

You are probably reading this book because you too lead God's people in worship. You want to do a good job, but might feel frustrated because your team's preparation and performance are sometimes sloppy, scattered, or less than their best.

We have met worship leaders who report leaving church with a feeling of disappointment. It is a feeling that they presented a well-intentioned, yet blemished, offering to the Lord.

We (the authors of this book) have been involved in church music ministries since we met in the late '70s. A few of these ministries have been in large churches with a paid staff of professional and highly trained musicians. However, most of our experiences have been in small- to moderate-sized churches, with music ministries staffed mostly by volunteers.

We have observed that contemporary praise and worship teams are usually comprised of highly motivated individuals with good hearts and a wide range of musical skills. This book is for these people.

The Praise and Worship Team Instant Tune-Up is not designed to teach you *how* to worship or *why* you should use a certain musical style. Nor is it designed to inspire you with a series of devotional and motivational messages. We have chosen to leave these very important issues to other writers. This book is about the equally important matters of how to organize and run a contemporary church music ministry.

This book assumes you are already involved in a praise and worship ministry. It also assumes you sometimes feel frustrated, guilty, or unorganized.

It has been our observation that often when people in worship ministry get frustrated with, feel guilty about, or seem unorganized with aspects of their praise and worship ministry, it is not because they have ungodly attitudes. It is mostly because they lack some of the organizational, musical, and/or leadership skills necessary to do a good job. If that describes you, this book will help you in those areas.

In this book you will find musical and leadership tips, tools, and tricks of the trade from the professionals that you can adapt and begin using right now. The book contains plenty of short, right-to-the-point bits of advice, as well as lengthier sections. Some of the things won't apply to you, but most will. It is also probable that you won't agree with everything in this book, which is okay.

Wherever you are on the musical skills continuum, you are sure to find ideas and resources that can have a real impact on your ministry.

We pray God's rich blessings on you and your ministry.

Now, let's get to work.

THiS BOOK IS aBOUt how to ORGaNIZe aND RUN a coNtemPORaRy ChURCh MUSIC MiNIS+RY.

chapteR 1

Give YouR PLAYiNG a TuNe-uP

in This chapter You WiLL LeaRn

- How to get that thick, professional sound with contemporary chord substitutions.
- Chord substitutions for keyboardists.
- Chord substitutions for guitarists.
- Easy ways to spice up your music by changing keys.
- Quick tips: do's and don'ts for players.

introDuction +o This chapter

This chapter is designed to help you be more like the musicians described in 1 Chronicles 25. In that passage, we are told the musicians who played at the house of God played skillfully.

"Played *skillfully*." We, like David, should insist that the band playing in the house of God be skillful. While there may be such a thing as musical gift-edness, you will find that most professional musicians agree that skillful playing is 1 percent inspiration and 99 percent perspiration.

Let's face it: There is a big difference between sounding like a sloppy garage band and sounding like a well-rehearsed, well-tuned team. Some people suggest that there are only three things you can do to give your playing a tune-up: practice, practice, and practice.

We *partly* agree. Of course you have to practice. We *all* have to practice. No one should expect to sound great on Sundays after letting their instrument sit idle and gather dust all week.

However, there are a number of tips, tricks, and "trade secrets" professional musicians use to help get that thick adult contemporary sound. All professional musicians use them. Whether they learned them playing in a nightclub trio before they came to Christ or picked them up at a church musician's conference, professional musicians have their little bag of tricks that sets their music apart.

> Get Ready to Learn a series of tips, musical tricks, and "trade secrets" that will give your playing a boost.

The good news for you is that most of these so-called trade secrets can be rather easy to learn! Sure, you'll have to work hard at first to "get them in your fingers," but you *can* learn them. Remember, there was a time when those professionals you admire so much didn't know them. One by one, they picked them up. Here's your opportunity.

Like the other chapters in this book, we will begin with several longer sections. You should work through the material in these longer sections slowly, carefully, and methodically. This is the material that will make a lasting impact on the way you do things, so take your time.

At the end of this chapter you will find a series of do's and don'ts for players. If you need a quick fix, fresh idea, or you just don't like details, this section is for you. Some of the ideas you'll agree with. Some you won't. But like it or not, this is the kind of material that effective contemporary musicians know and put into practice.

How to Get That Thick, Professional Sound with Contemporary Chord Substitutions

If you have spent any time listening to contemporary praise and worship musicians play, you no doubt noticed their music sounds big. Then, like all of us, you went out and purchased praise and worship songbooks, started playing from them, and suddenly noticed something. Your music didn't quite sound the same. In fact, even though you played exactly what was written in the songbook, your playing sounded sort of insubstantial and thin.

Here's why: Many (if not most) professional musicians rarely play plain old major, minor, and seventh chords. They play chord substitutions instead. In other words, although the music calls for a D chord, seasoned musicians often substitute something else like D Major9 2nd inversion.

So why doesn't the music call for a D Major9 2nd inversion? Companies that publish songbooks know that most people who buy songbooks have no idea what a D Major9 2nd inversion is, so they print the plain old D chord. That plain old D chord will work, it just sounds . . . well, plain.

Ready for some great news? This book is going to show you scads of those secret fat chords the pros use. You will find two parts here—one for keyboardists and one for guitarists.

Someone once said, "Learning and using new chords is like getting new shoes: They are uncomfortable at first, but then you break them in and before you know it they feel great!"

D CHORD? i DON't think So. i think i'LL PLAY a D6+9 iNStEaD!

Now before you glance ahead, read this carefully: *Go slow.* Take your time. Don't try to learn too many at once. Remember, that plain old D chord has served you pretty well all these years.

Before you start using chord substitutions during worship, you must make sure you can nail them. You must be able to play them cleanly, perfectly, without thinking, and without hesitation. When you drive your car, you don't have to pause and look to see where the brake pedal is. *You just know.* That is the way your chord substitutions have to be before you go public. If you can't snatch them spontaneously, wait.

Test Your Readiness

Make a set of flash cards. It may sound childish, but there is no better way to drill. Here is what you do: Put the names of the chords you are learning on cards, mix them up, then spread them out and try to play them in a rapid succession. Keep this book nearby for reference in case you need to peek. Look at the following illustration.

DON't DaRE GO PUBLIC WITH YOUR NEW CHORDS UNtiL YOU have them DOWN COLD.

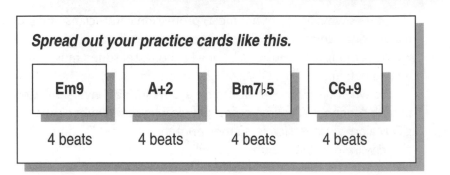

Spread out your practice cards like this.

Em9	A+2	Bm7♭5	C6+9
4 beats	4 beats	4 beats	4 beats

As you drill your new chords, it is a good idea to work with a metronome or drum machine. The absolute, undisputed best way to master your new chords is to slow the tempo down to a crawl. Then, ever so gradually, move the speed up notch by notch.

Learning new chords is frustrating for many people. However, if you practice slowly at first, incrementally increasing the tempo, you will develop what is known as "muscle memory." In other words, your fingers will seem to develop a mind of their own that enables them to grab those flashy new chords effortlessly.

ChORD SuBStitutioNS FOR KeYBoaRDiStS

Everybody knows when it comes to playing keyboards, it's different strokes for different folks. You might be a classically trained piano major with a broad and deep understanding of music theory. On the other hand, some of you have studied jazz, and you know your intervals and scales inside and out. Not you? Maybe you are the kind of player who knows a few chords, kind of watches the music, and improvises her way through, or perhaps you just play by ear.

The ideas included in this chapter are designed to help you wherever you are along the musical skill continuum. First, we will explain the ideas, then we will show you what notes to play.

Take your time. Be patient with yourself. There is only one magic formula for improving your playing—practice!

The Big Idea Is Adding Secret Ingredients

We love to grill food. Take hamburgers for example. While it is fine to take some ground beef, make patties, and slap them on the grill, that won't do at our house. Whenever we grill hamburgers, we use two secret ingredients. First, we mince a few slices of onion. Then we get some Worcestershire sauce and gently fold the ingredients into the ground beef. We automatically do it this way every time. The idea of serving plain hamburger just isn't a part of our culinary experience. When we serve these hamburgers to guests, they consistently ask, "Why don't the hamburgers I cook at home taste like these?" Doug and I just smile at each other and shrug our shoulders.

You get the idea. Simple additions make a noticeable difference. Want to make your music sound bigger and thicker? Add one or more notes to the basic chords in your music. It is that simple.

For example, whenever you see a major chord in the music, play the major, but add a secret ingredient to it: the 2nd. Didn't sound quite right in your song? Try a different ingredient instead: add in the 6th. Some of you reading right now have no idea what a 2nd or 6th is. Relax, because we will spell it out for you in the charts that follow.

For those of you who *do* play by chord symbols, get used to these basic principles:

Major Chords

Automatically add in one of these—the 2nd, 6th, or Major 7th. Just get used to doing it. Trust your ears, and you are likely to find that adding the 2nd should become your de facto standard when playing contemporary music.

Minor Chords

Automatically add in the dominant 7th and/or the 2nd. For example, Em becomes Em7+2. Your chords will always sound bigger this way, and you can play this alongside a plain minor chord. So if your guitarist can't handle it, let him play the plain minor while you blend in the 7th and 2nd. It will sound fine because your added notes—secret ingredients—embellish the cord.

Dominant 7th Chords

Automatically add in the 2nd for more thickness, or try flatting the 9th for a sassier sound.

Before you know it, only playing plain major, minor, and dominant 7th chords will gradually disappear from your musical vocabulary. Ready to get specific?

How to Use the Keyboard Charts

Let's get down to business and take some of these chords for a test drive! Carry this book to your keyboard or piano. Continue reading until we get to the charts. If you are new to these chords, they might feel and sound a little awkward at first. Stick with them. You will find as you start using them, you will begin wondering how you ever lived without them.

At the top of each section you will see the standard chord (with the notes spelled out) found in most music songbooks. Just below this you will find one or more basic substitutions. Below this, a more advanced one, and finally at the end a more esoteric one to experiment with. Play the root in the minus one and minus two positions with your left hand as you try each chord. Keep trying them in your music until you find ones that fit. Have fun!

Following the first chord of each chord type, there is a musical example in chord chart format. Play through the example trying each suggested substitution, and listen to how the music sounds different with the embellished or altered substitute chords.

Keyboard Substitution Charts

Major Chords

Embellishing major chords is one of the easiest things you can do to give your playing a tune-up. Make it your goal to get a feel for the sound of each of the different types of substitutions below. Hint: Don't limit yourself to playing the right-hand notes in the order presented. If it doesn't sound right or feels uncomfortable on your hands, try a different inversion (i.e., try moving the bottom note to the top of the chord).

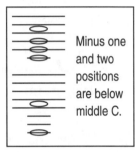

Minus one and two positions are below middle C.

C Major

Written:	C	(C, E, G)	*Yawn.*
Try this:	C2	(C, D, E, G)	*Thumb on C and D. Sounds richer.*
Or this:	C6	(C, E, G, A)	*Popular with country styles.*
Or this:	Cmaj7	(C, E, G, B)	*Jazzy, silky, smooth.*
Or this:	Cmaj9	(E, G, B, D)	*LH plays root. Very jazzy.*
If you dare!	C6+9	(E, G, A, D)	*LH plays root. Yow!*

Example Chord Progression (Note the suggested C chord substitutions below.)
Play each chord for four quarter notes. Play the root in the left hand.

Chord: ‖: C / / / |G / / / |Am / / / |Em / / / |F / / / |G / / / :‖
Notes to play: [C, E, G]   [B, D, G]   [A, C, E]   [G, B, E]   [A,C,F]   [G, B, D]

Now, try it with the following substitutes

Chord: ‖:C2 / / / |G / / / |Am / / / |Em / / / |F / / / |G / / / :‖
Notes to play: [C, D, E, G] [B, D, G]   [A, C, E]   [G, B, E]   [A, C, F]   [G, B, D]
Chord: ‖:Cmaj7 / / / |G / / / |Am / / / |Em / / / |F / / / |G / / / :‖
Notes to play: [C, E, G, B]   [B, D, G]   [A, C, E]   [G, B, E]   [A, C, F]   [G, B, D]

After you have reviewed the rest of the charts, and you are ready for something advanced, try the following. Remember keep the root in the left hand. You will learn about the final 13♭9 chord later in the chapter.

Chord: ‖:Cmaj9 / / / |G2 / / / |Am2+7 / / / |Em11 / / / ‖Fmaj7 / / / |G13♭9 / / / :‖
Notes to play: [B, D, E, G]   [A, B, D, G] [G, A, B, C, E] [G, A, B, D, F♯][F, A, C, E]   [A♭, B, D, E, F]

D♭ Major
Written:	D♭	(D♭, F, A♭)	*Same as C♯.*
Try this:	D♭2	(D♭, E♭, F, A♭)	*Sounds richer.*
Or this:	D♭6	(D♭, F, A♭, B♭)	*Popular with country styles.*
Or this:	D♭maj7	(D♭, F, A♭, C)	*Jazzy, silky, smooth.*
Or this:	D♭maj9	(F, A♭, C, E♭)	*LH plays root. Very jazzy.*
If you dare:	D♭6+9	(F, A♭, B♭, E♭)	*LH plays root. Oh yes!*

D Major
Written:	D	(D, F♯, A)	*Zzzz.*
Try this:	D2	(D, E, F♯, A)	*Sounds richer.*
Or this:	D6	(D, F♯, A, B)	*Popular with country styles.*
Or this:	Dmaj7	(D, F♯, A, C♯)	*Jazzy, silky, smooth.*
Or this:	Dmaj9	(F♯, A, C♯, E)	*LH plays root. Very jazzy.*
If you dare:	D6+9	(F♯, A, B, E)	*LH plays root.*

E♭ Major
Written:	E♭	(E♭, G, B♭)	*Same as D♯.*
Try this:	E♭2	(E♭, F, G, B♭)	*Sounds richer.*
Or this:	E♭6	(E♭, G, B♭, C)	*Popular with country styles.*
Or this:	E♭maj7	(E♭, G, B♭, D)	*Jazzy, silky, smooth.*
Or this:	E♭maj9	(G, B♭, D, F)	*LH plays root. Very jazzy.*
If you dare:	E♭6+9	(G, B♭, C, F)	*LH plays root.*

F Major
Written:	F	(F, A, C)	*Plain Jane.*
Try this:	F2	(F, G, A, C)	*Sounds richer.*
Or this:	F6	(F, A, C, D)	*Popular with country styles.*
Or this:	Fmaj7	(F, A, C, E)	*Jazzy, silky, smooth.*
Or this:	Fmaj9	(A, C, E, G)	*LH plays root. Very jazzy.*
If you dare:	F6+9	(A, C, D, G)	*LH plays root.*

F# Major

Written:	F#	(F#, A#, C#)	*Same as Gb.*
Try this:	F#2	(F#, G#, A#, C#)	*Sounds richer.*
Or this:	F#6	(F#, A#, C#, D#)	*Popular with country styles.*
Or this:	F#maj7	(F#, A#, C#, F)	*Jazzy, silky, smooth.*
Or this:	F#maj9	(A#, C#, F, G#)	*LH plays root. Very jazzy.*
If you dare:	F#6+9	(A#, C#, D#, G#)	*LH plays root.*

G Major

Written:	G	(G, B, D)	*Wake me up when . . .*
Try this:	G2	(G, A, B, D)	*Sounds richer.*
Or this:	G6	(G, B, D, E)	*Popular with country styles.*
Or this:	Gmaj7	(G, B, D, F#)	*Jazzy, silky, smooth.*
Or this:	Gmaj9	(B, D, F#, A)	*LH plays root. Very jazzy.*
If you dare:	G6+9	(B, D, E, A)	*LH plays root.*

Ab Major

Written:	Ab	(Ab, C, Eb)	*Same as G#.*
Try this:	Ab2	(Ab, Bb, C, Eb)	*Sounds richer.*
Or this:	Ab6	(Ab, C, Eb, F)	*Popular with country styles.*
Or this:	Abmaj7	(Ab, C, Eb, G)	*Jazzy, silky, smooth.*
Or this:	Abmaj9	(C, Eb, G, Bb)	*LH plays root. Very jazzy.*
If you dare:	Ab6+9	(C, Eb, F, Bb)	*LH plays root.*

A Major

Written:	A	(A, C#, E)	*Zzzz.*
Try this:	A2	(A, B, C#, E)	*Sounds richer.*
Or this:	A6	(A, C#, E, F#)	*Popular with country styles.*
Or this:	Amaj7	(A, C#, E, G#)	*Jazzy, silky, smooth.*
Or this:	Amaj9	(C#, E, G#, B)	*LH plays root. Very jazzy.*
If you dare:	A6+9	(C#, E, F#, B)	*LH plays root.*

Bb Major

Written:	Bb	(Bb, D, F)	*Same as A#.*
Try this:	Bb2	(Bb, C, D, F)	*Sounds richer.*
Or this:	Bb6	(Bb, D, F, G)	*Popular with country styles.*
Or this:	Bbmaj7	(Bb, D, F, A)	*Jazzy, silky, smooth.*
Or this:	Bbmaj9	(D, F, A, C)	*LH plays root. Very jazzy.*
If you dare:	Bb6+9	(D, F, G, C)	*LH plays root.*

B Major

Written:	B	(B, D♯, F♯)	Bland.
Try this:	B2	(B, C♯, D♯, F♯)	Sounds richer.
Or this:	B6	(B, D♯, F♯, G♯)	Popular with country styles.
Or this:	Bmaj7	(B, D♯, F♯, A♯)	Jazzy, silky, smooth.
Or this:	Bmaj9	(D♯, F♯, A♯, C♯)	LH plays root. Very jazzy.
If you dare:	B6+9	(D♯, F♯, G♯, C♯)	LH plays root.

Seventh Chords

Substituting alternates for your seventh chords is a great way to give your playing "attitude." By all means, you must learn the 9th, then experiment with some of the others. Some will sound better if substituted for only half the duration of the chord. In other words, if the music calls for a C7 for 4 beats, play a C7sus4 for two, then resolve to the regular C7.

C7

Written:	C7	(C, E, G, B♭)	Yawn.
Try this:	C9	(E, G, B♭, D)	LH plays root. Sounds bigger.
Or this:	C11	(G, B♭, D, F)	LH plays root. Sounds even bigger.
Or this:	C7sus4	(G, B♭, C, F)	Should resolve to C7.
Or this:	C7♭9	(G, B♭, D♭, E)	Resolve to C7.
If you dare:	C7♯5	(C, E, G♯, B♭)	Sassy.

Example Chord Progression (Note the suggested C chord substitutions below.)
Play each chord for four quarter notes. Play the root in the left hand.

Chord: ‖F / / / |B♭ / / / |C7 / / / ‖F / / / ‖
Notes to play: [A, C, F]   [F, B♭, D]   [G, B♭ ,C, E] [A, C, F]

Now, try it with the following substitutes

Chord: ‖F / / / |B♭ / / / |C9 / / / ‖F / / / ‖
Notes to play: [A, C, F]   [F, B♭, D]   [G, B♭, D, E] [A, C, F]

Chord: ‖F / / / |B♭ / / / |C7sus4 /   C7 /   ‖F / / / ‖
Notes to play: [A, C, F]   [F, B♭, D]   [G, B♭, C, F]   [G, B♭, C, E] [A, C, F]

D♭7

Written:	D♭7	(D♭, F, A♭, C♭)	Yawn.
Try this:	D♭9	(F, A♭, C♭, E♭)	LH plays root. Sounds bigger.
Or this:	D♭11	(A♭, C♭, E♭, G♭)	LH plays root. Sounds even bigger.
Or this:	D♭7sus4	(A♭, C♭, D♭, G♭)	Should resolve to D♭7.
Or this:	D♭7♭9	(F, A♭, C♭, D)	Resolve to D♭7.
If you dare:	D♭7♯5	(F, A, C♭, D♭)	Sassy.

D7

Written:	D7	(D, F#, A, C)	Yawn.
Try this:	D9	(F#, A, C, E)	LH plays root. Sounds bigger.
Or this:	D11	(A, C, E, G)	LH plays root. Sounds even bigger.
Or this:	D7sus4	(A, C, D, G)	Should resolve to D7.
Or this:	D7b9	(F#, A, C, Eb)	Resolve to D7.
If you dare:	D7#5	(F#, A#, C, D)	Sassy.

Eb7

Written:	Eb7	(Eb, G, Bb, Db)	Yawn.
Try this:	Eb9	(G, Bb, Db, F)	LH plays root. Sounds bigger.
Or this:	Eb11	(Bb, Db, F, Ab)	LH plays root. Sounds even bigger.
Or this:	Eb7sus4	(Bb, Db, Eb, Ab)	Should resolve to Eb7.
Or this:	Eb7b9	(G, Bb, Db, E)	Resolve to Eb7.
If you dare:	Eb7#5	(G, B, Db, Eb)	Sassy.

E7

Written:	E7	(E, G#, B, D)	Yawn.
Try this:	E9	(G#, B, D, F#)	LH plays root. Sounds bigger.
Or this:	E11	(B, D, F#, A)	LH plays root. Sounds even bigger.
Or this:	E7sus4	(B, D, E, A)	Should resolve to E7.
Or this:	E7b9	(G#, B, D, F)	Resolve to E7.
If you dare:	E7#5	(G#, C, D, E)	Sassy.

F7

Written:	F7	(F, A, C, Eb)	Yawn.
Try this:	F9	(A, C, Eb, G)	LH plays root. Sounds bigger.
Or this:	F11	(C, Eb, G, Bb)	LH plays root. Sounds even bigger.
Or this:	F7sus4	(C, Eb, F, Bb)	Should resolve to F7.
Or this:	F7b9	(A, C, Eb, Gb)	Resolve to F7.
If you dare:	F7#5	(F, A, Db, Eb)	Sassy.

F#7

Written:	F#7	(F#, A#, C#, E)	Yawn. Same as Gb.
Try this:	F#9	(A#, C#, E, G#)	LH plays root. Sounds bigger.
Or this:	F11	(C#, E, G#, B)	LH plays root. Sounds even bigger.
Or this:	F7sus4	(C#, E, F#, B)	Should resolve to F#7.
Or this:	F7b9	(A#, C#, E, G)	Resolve to F#7.
If you dare:	F7#5	(F#, A#, D, E)	Sassy.

G7

Written:	G7	(G, B, D, F)	*Yawn.*
Try this:	G9	(B, D, F, A)	*LH plays root. Sounds bigger.*
Or this:	G11	(D, F, A, C)	*LH plays root. Sounds even bigger.*
Or this:	G7sus4	(D, F, G, C)	*Should resolve to G7.*
Or this:	G7♭9	(B, D, F, A♭)	*Resolve to G7.*
If you dare:	G7♯5	(G, B, D♯, F)	*Sassy.*

A♭7

Written:	A♭7	(A♭, C, E♭, G♭)	*Same as G♯.*
Try this:	A♭9	(C, E♭, G♭, B♭)	*LH plays root. Sounds bigger.*
Or this:	A♭11	(E♭, G♭, B♭, D♭)	*LH plays root. Sounds even bigger.*
Or this:	A♭7sus4	(E♭, G♭, A♭, D♭)	*Should resolve to A♭7.*
Or this:	A♭7♭9	(B♭, E♭, G♭, A)	*Resolve to A♭7.*
If you dare:	A♭7♯5	(A♭, C, E, G♭)	*Sassy.*

A7

Written:	A7	(A, C♯, E, G)	*Yawn.*
Try this:	A9	(C♯, E, G, B)	*LH plays root. Sounds bigger.*
Or this:	A11	(E, G, B♯, D)	*LH plays root. Sounds even bigger.*
Or this:	A7sus4	(D, E, G, A)	*Should resolve to A7.*
Or this:	A7♭9	(C♯, E, G, B♭)	*Resolve to A7.*
If you dare:	A7♯5	(A, C♯, F, G)	*Sassy.*

B♭7

Written:	B♭7	(B♭, D, F, A♭)	*Yawn.*
Try this:	B♭9	(D, F, A♭, C)	*LH plays root. Sounds bigger.*
Or this:	B♭11	(F, A♭, C, E♭)	*LH plays root. Sounds even bigger.*
Or this:	B♭7sus4	(E♭, F, A♭, B♭)	*Should resolve to B♭7.*
Or this:	B♭7b9	(D, F, A♭, B)	*Resolve to B♭7.*
If you dare:	B♭7♯5	(B♭, D, G♭, A)	*Sassy.*

B7

Written:	B7	(B, D♯, F♯, A)	*Yawn.*
Try this:	B9	(D♯, F♯, A, C♯)	*LH plays root. Sounds bigger.*
Or this:	B11	(F♯, A, D♯, E)	*LH plays root. Sounds even bigger.*
Or this:	B7sus4	(E, F♯, A, B)	*Should resolve to B7.*
Or this:	B7♭9	(D♯, F♯, A, C)	*Resolve to B7.*
If you dare:	B7♯5	(B, D♯, G, A♯)	*Sassy.*

Minor Chords

Substituted minor chords will be some of your most beautiful and richly textured sounds. Don't play them ostentatiously—keep them subtle.

Cm

Written:	Cm	(C, E♭, G)	*Yawn.*
Try this:	Cm7	(C, E♭, G, B♭)	*Good for up tempo.*
Or this:	Cm2	(C, D, E♭, G)	*Mysterious, for slow songs.*
Or this:	Cm6	(C, E♭, G, A)	*Hollow sounding.*
Or this:	Cm9	(E♭, G, B♭, D)	*LH plays root. Smooth jazz.*
If you dare:	Cm11	(B♭, D, E♭, F, G)	*LH plays root. Devastating.*

Example Chord Progression (Note the suggested C chord substitutions below.)
Play each chord for four quarter notes. Play the root in the left hand.

Chord: ‖:Cm / / / |B♭ / / / |A♭ / / / |Gm / / /:‖
Notes to play: [G, C, E♭] [F, B♭, D] [A♭, C, E♭] [G, B♭, D]

Now, try it with the following substitutes.

Chord: ‖:Cm7 / / / |B♭ / / / |A♭ / / / |Gm7 / / /:‖
Notes to play: [G, B♭, C, E♭] [F, B♭, D] [A♭, C, E♭] [G, B♭, D, F]

Let's take it up a notch.

Chord: ‖:Cm9 / / / |B♭2 / / / |A♭maj7 / / / |Gm9 / / /:‖
Notes to play: [G, B♭, D, E♭] [F, B♭, C, D] [A♭, C, E♭, G] [A, B♭, D, F]

One last time.

Chord: ‖:Cm11 / / / |B♭2 / / / |A♭maj9 / / / |Gm11 / / /:‖
Notes to play: [G, B♭, D, E♭, F] [F, B♭, C, D] [B♭, C, E♭, G] [A, B♭, C, D, F]

D♭m

Written:	D♭m	(D♭, E, A♭)	*Yawn.*
Try this:	D♭m7	(D♭, E, A♭, B)	*Good for up tempo.*
Or this:	D♭m2	(D♭, E♭, E, A♭)	*Mysterious, for slow songs.*
Or this:	D♭m6	(D♭, E, A♭, B♭)	*Hollow sounding.*
Or this:	D♭m9	(E, A♭, B, E♭)	*LH plays root. Smooth jazz.*
If you dare:	D♭m11	(B, E♭, E, G♭, A♭)	*LH plays root. Devastating.*

Dm

Written:	Dm	(D, F, A)	Yawn.
Try this:	Dm7	(D, F, A, C)	Good for up tempo.
Or this:	Dm2	(D, E, F, A)	Mysterious, for slow songs.
Or this:	Dm6	(D, F, A, B)	Hollow sounding.
Or this:	Dm9	(F, A, C, E)	LH plays root. Smooth jazz.
If you dare:	Dm11	(C, E, F, G, A)	LH plays root. Devastating.

E♭m

Written:	E♭m	(E♭, G♭, B♭)	Yawn.
Try this:	E♭m7	(E♭, G♭, B♭, D♭)	Good for up tempo.
Or this:	E♭m2	(E♭, F, G♭, B♭)	Mysterious, for slow songs.
Or this:	E♭m6	(E♭, G♭, B♭, C)	Hollow sounding.
Or this:	E♭m9	(G♭, B♭, D♭, F)	LH plays root. Smooth jazz.
If you dare:	E♭m11	(D♭, F, G♭, A♭, B♭)	LH plays root. Devastating.

Em

Written:	Em	(E, G, B)	Yawn.
Try this:	Em7	(E, G, B, D)	Good for up tempo.
Or this:	Em2	(E, F♯, G, B)	Mysterious, for slow songs.
Or this:	Em6	(E, G, B, C♯)	Hollow sounding.
Or this:	Em9	(G, B, D, F♯)	LH plays root. Smooth jazz.
If you dare:	Em11	(D, F♯, G, A, B)	LH plays root. Devastating.

Fm

Written:	Fm	(F, A♭, C)	Yawn.
Try this:	Fm7	(F, A♭, C, E♭)	Good for up tempo.
Or this:	Fm2	(F, G, A♭, C)	Mysterious, for slow songs.
Or this:	Fm6	(F, A♭, C, D)	Hollow sounding.
Or this:	Fm9	(A♭, C, E♭, G)	LH plays root. Smooth jazz.
If you dare:	Fm11	(E♭, G, E♭, D)	LH plays root. Devastating.

F♯m

Written:	F♯m	(F♯, A, C♯)	Yawn.
Try this:	F♯m7	(F♯, A, C♯, E)	Good for up tempo.
Or this:	F♯m2	(F♯, G♯, A, C♯)	Mysterious, for slow songs.
Or this:	F♯m6	(F♯, A, C♯, D♯)	Hollow sounding.
Or this:	F♯m9	(A, C♯, E, G♯)	LH plays root. Smooth jazz.
If you dare:	F♯m11	(A, C, C♯, E, G♯)	LH plays root. Devastating.

Gm

Written:	Gm	(G, B♭, D)	*Yawn.*
Try this:	Gm7	(G, B♭, D, F)	*Good for up tempo.*
Or this:	Gm2	(G, A, B♭, D)	*Mysterious, for slow songs.*
Or this:	Gm6	(G, B♭, D, E)	*Hollow sounding.*
Or this:	Gm9	(B♭, D, F, A)	*LH plays root. Smooth jazz.*
If you dare:	Gm11	(A, B♭, C♯, D, F)	*LH plays root. Devastating.*

A♭m

Written:	A♭m	(A♭, B, E♭)	*Yawn.*
Try this:	A♭m7	(A♭, B, E♭, G♭)	*Good for up tempo.*
Or this:	A♭m2	(A♭, B♭, B, E♭)	*Mysterious, for slow songs.*
Or this:	A♭m6	(A♭, B, E♭, F)	*Hollow sounding.*
Or this:	A♭m9	(B, E♭, G♭, B♭)	*LH plays root. Smooth jazz.*
If you dare:	A♭m11	(B♭, B, D, E♭, G♭)	*LH plays root. Devastating.*

Am

Written:	Am	(A, C, E)	*Yawn.*
Try this:	Am7	(A, C, E, G)	*Good for up tempo.*
Or this:	Am2	(A, B, C, E)	*Mysterious, for slow songs.*
Or this:	Am6	(A, C, E, F♯)	*Hollow sounding.*
Or this:	Am9	(C, E, G, B)	*LH plays root. Smooth jazz.*
If you dare:	Am11	(B, C, D, E, G)	*LH plays root. Devastating.*

B♭m

Written:	B♭m	(B♭, D♭, F)	*Yawn.*
Try this:	B♭m7	(B♭, D♭, F, A♭)	*Good for up tempo.*
Or this:	B♭m2	(B♭, C, D♭, F)	*Mysterious, for slow songs.*
Or this:	B♭m6	(B♭, D♭, F, G)	*Hollow sounding.*
Or this:	B♭m9	(D♭, F, A♭, C)	*LH plays root. Smooth jazz.*
If you dare:	B♭m11	(F, A♭, C, D♭, E♭)	*LH plays root. Devastating.*

Bm

Written:	Bm	(B, D, F♯)	*Yawn.*
Try this:	Bm7	(B, D, F♯, A)	*Good for up tempo.*
Or this:	Bm2	(B, C♯, D, F♯)	*Mysterious, for slow songs.*
Or this:	Bm6	(B, D, F♯, G♯)	*Hollow sounding.*
Or this:	Bm9	(D, F♯, A, C♯)	*LH plays root. Smooth jazz.*
If you dare:	Bm11	(F♯, A, C♯, D, E)	*LH plays root. Devastating.*

How Do I Know What to Substitute?

If you are new to this type of playing, you might be thinking: *Okay, these chords do sound a little different, but how do I know whether to substitute a major 9th or a 6th?*

The answer is to let your ears be your guide. There are no hard-and-fast rules. Some players favor the 6th over the 2nd for example. Both will work and will almost certainly sound better than the plain triad chord. But which one *you* use is a matter of personal taste. However, when you substitute, you might want to keep these principles in mind:

1. Substitute consistently. If you start substituting for a given chord, your song will usually sound better if you use the same substitution throughout the song. For example, if you substitute a Dmaj7 chord for a D chord, you should probably always substitute the Dmaj7 for the D throughout the song.

2. Whenever possible, match substitutions with other players. In other words, if you play keyboards and you plan to substitute an E♭maj9 for an E♭, try to get your guitarist to do the same. If for some reason your guitarist can't pull it off, that's usually okay because most of the substitutions suggested in the substitution charts can be played on top of the plain chords. This is true for all but the most exotic ones. So, for example, if you play a G2 on keyboards and your guitar player plays a plain old G chord, it will sound just fine.

As stated, you *don't* want different players substituting differently. In other words, you don't want an Em2 on keyboards while your guitarist plays Em6+9. That usually causes bad dissonance. Here's what the pros do: During rehearsals, simply announce that you're playing Em2 instead of Em. All other players covering chords should play either the plain Em or Em2, but *not* any other substitutions. It's just too risky.

3. Hearing a clash? You may find on some of the more exotic chords something is just not right. In these cases, you might try dropping a note. This is fine, as long as you drop the right one. These are the three immutable rules for dropping notes.

1. If you're playing the 9th, ♭9th, or ♯9th, *drop the root in the right hand.*
2. If you're playing sus2 or sus4, *drop the 3rd in the right hand.*
3. If you're playing ♭5th, ♯5th, ♯11th, or 13th, *drop the 5th in the right hand.*

One final note, if your singers like to harmonize, listen carefully as you substitute chords. In the same way that a guitar and piano can clash when mixing substitutions, you can also clash with your altos if, for example, you flat a 9th and they don't.

Chord Substitutions for Guitarists

In 1 Corinthians 13:11, the apostle Paul says, "When I was a child, I talked like a child, I thought like a child, I reasoned like a child. When I became a man, I put childish ways behind me."

If Paul was a guitar player he might have said, "When I was a guitar beginner, I played kiddie chords. When I became a praise and worship leader, I put childish guitar chords behind me."

What Grade Are You In?

When I (Doug) am teaching guitar chords, I like to tell my students that there are different levels of playing, all of which are important during the learning process. Learning guitar playing is like learning any other complicated topic. You need to crawl before you walk, and walk before you run. But let's face it: Running is a lot more fun than crawling. Let's learn to run!

I like to help students think of guitar chords in three broad categories I correlate to different levels of education: kiddie chords, high school chords, and college chords. Let's briefly look at each.

Kiddie Chords

These are the basics. If someone wants to learn guitar, these are the chords they will cut their teeth on. They are all played below the fourth fret, and they don't require more than three fingers.

The essential assortment of kiddie chords includes

E, Em, E7, Em7
A, Am, A7, Am7
D, Dm, D7
G, G7
C, C7
F, F7
B7, Bm

I trust you can play every one of these without even thinking. Since tens of thousands of songs have been composed using kiddie chords, many guitarists learn these basics and never go beyond them. That's fine for them, *but not for you.*

High School Chords

Guitarists who are content with kiddie chords often go kicking and screaming into high school when someone asks them to play a F#m7. High school chords are also known as, you guessed it, *bar chords*. Bar chords get their name because you use your index finger to hold down all six strings at once, thus "barring," or preventing notes below the bar from sounding.

Of course, you don't want to be like the guitarists who only know five or six bar chords. Learn them all! The wonderful thing about bar chords is, once you know eight of them, you can play in *any* key! Learn bar chords and you'll never flinch when someone asks you to play an E♭m7.

We won't take time here to cover bar chords. The point is that you need to know them. If you don't, go to school.

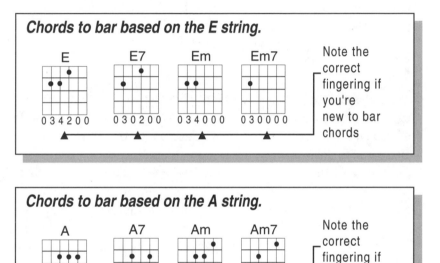

You say you don't like bar chords? Before you use the excuse "I can't play those chords on my guitar—I get nothing but buzz" or if bar chords just plain hurt, recognize that you have a few options.

1. Get a set of lighter gauge strings. This alone can make you feel as if you have a new instrument.
2. Take your guitar to a reputable guitar shop and tell them you want the "action" improved. The action refers to the distance between your strings and the fretboard. On many guitars this is adjustable. Pay the fifty dollars and start learning bar chords.
3. Best of all, here's the excuse you've been looking for to justify buying a new instrument!

When it is time to replace your instrument, forget about finding one that looks cool or buying one on name recognition alone. We have seen plenty of examples of well-known and expensive guitars that are absolute beasts to play. Go first for the feel.

When you arrive at the guitar store, play as many guitars as you can get your hands on. Seriously. Play at least ten different guitars. As you do, get brutally honest and ask yourself how each one feels in your hands. When you find one or two you like, try out some of those chords you were never able to play cleanly on your old guitar. Can you nail them? If so, buy it.

Remember this sage advice: A good guitar shouldn't fight you when you play it. If a salesperson starts talking about "breaking an instrument in" or "developing new muscles" in your hands and arms, kindly hand the instrument back and shop elsewhere. Get a guitar that works for you.

College Chords

Did you go to college after high school? If so, hopefully your postsecondary experience was a time to explore new ideas, expand your horizons, learn as much as you could from others, *while* you developed your own intellectual framework and core life skills.

If you are the kind of guitar player who wants to move up musically, you will soon tire of kiddie and high school chords. Sure, you will continue to use the basic and bar chords, but sooner or later, you'll see someone, somewhere playing her guitar when she hits a chord that simply sounds magical! Suddenly you will notice something inside you says: *Whoah! Dude! Show me how you played that!*

A GOOD GUITAR SHOULDN'T FIGHT YOU WHEN YOU PLAY IT.

College chords are the alternates and the substitutes, those subtle, unusual, yet extremely interesting chords that make people sit up and take notice. They make your music rise above the status quo. They can show up anywhere on the fretboard and always sound great. And here is the great news: Many of them are really not that difficult to play!

There are literally thousands of college chords you can learn. In this book, we will introduce you to some of the basic, yet very cool chords that separate the babies from the grown-ups. Remember, you will rarely substitute *every* chord in a song. The skilled artist instead subtly slides one in here and there to give their music shazaam.

Some of the Best College Chords

Here they are: On the left side of each chart you will find some of the most common kiddie chords used in today's music. To the right you will find one or more alternatives, more interesting chords that usually work as awesome substitutes. When you encounter a kiddie chord in your worship music, try slipping in one of the alternates and see how it sounds. If you are new to these chords, they might feel and sound a little awkward at first. Stick with them. Once you start using them, you will begin wondering how you ever managed to play without them. Following the charts, there are several music examples in lead sheet format. Play through all the examples and try to listen to how the music sounds different. By the way, the majority of the following alternate and embellished chords allow you to strum five or six strings.

MAJOR CHORD SUBSTITUTIONS

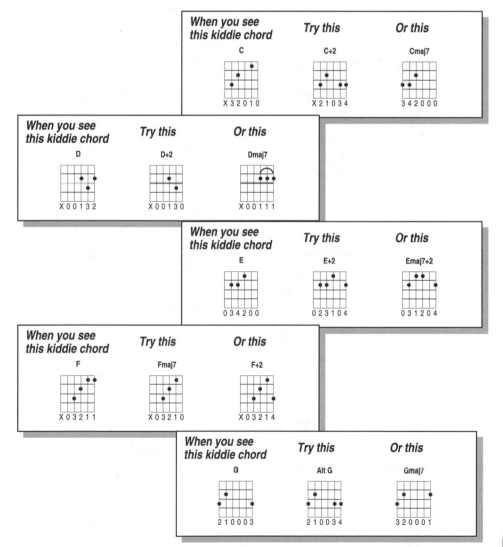

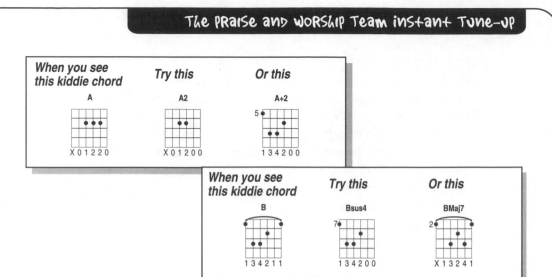

Minor Chord Substitutions

Switching out minor chords can make your music sound incredibly rich and thick. Here are several favorite embellishments for common minor chords.

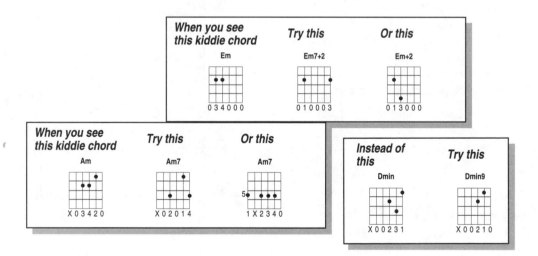

Seventh Chord Substitutions

Let's finish with a few favorite dominant seventh chord substitutions. These tend to sound great on faster songs.

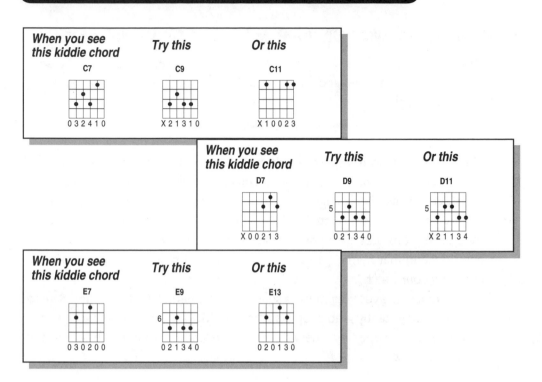

Once you get a sense for the ways the above substitutions and embellishments make your music sound and feel different, you can get instructional books with titles like *The Encyclopedia of Guitar Chords* and *1001 Guitar Chords* to help you figure out ways to play interesting chord substitutions in any key. If you don't want to pay for an instructional book, there are also dozens of Internet sites covering the same types of material where you can get the content for free! Just type "guitar chords" into your search engine and have a blast!

A well-known guitarist once picked up a guitar and said something like this:

> These things are amazing. There's so much music in them—you've got just six
> [strings] this way and twelve [frets] that way. Millions of people play 'em and
> yet people are still pulling all kinds of new things out of them. The guitar is an
> amazing instrument!

We couldn't agree more. Now that you have begun learning how to enhance your playing with chord substitutions, let's build upon that skill another way—key changes.

easy ways To spice up youR music By changing keys

Often, worship leaders string together a series of short songs into a medley, switching keys between and/or in the middle of songs. This changing of keys is called modulation.

Why Modulate?

There is a good reason why you should modulate occasionally—it makes your music more interesting. In fact, modulation can make your music downright exciting.

Have you ever been singing a hymn, one of those pieces with what seems like twenty verses all in the same key? Did you find your mind wandering after the third verse? Chances are if your music director would have modulated twice or even once in that hymn, you would have focused more on the lyrics than on checking your watch.

Modulation gives your music a sense of movement. When you modulate to a new key, you instantly grab people's attention. Moving up to a slightly higher key feels like you are opening a new door. It is like shifting from fourth to fifth gear. Let's learn how.

Modulation: Movin' on Up

When you modulate, you will usually move up from a lower key to a higher key. You might go up a half step, (for example from D to E♭), a whole step (C to D), or even up several intervals (D to G). Modulating up makes the verse in the new key seem brighter, happier, more powerful, and full of hope.

Here's an example of how modulating between verses can really make an impact:

Consider the hymn "How Great Thou Art."

Verse 1 in key of B♭   "Oh Lord my God, when I in awesome wonder . . ."
Verse 2 in key of B♭   "When through the woods, and forest glades I wander . . ."
Verse 3 in key of C   "And when I think, that God his Son not sparing . . ."
Verse 4 in key of D   "When Christ shall come, with shout of acclamation . . ."

Arranging the hymn this way would give verse three a bigger feel. Then, modulating again on the fourth verse would provide a triumphant feel.

Modulation: Downshifting

While less common, it is also acceptable to gradually work down to a lower key. You can do this when you are deliberately trying to calm or quiet your worshipers into a spirit of meditation and hush. You must be careful modulating down though, because it can sometimes feel that successive verses in lower keys are becoming more depressing. In the next chapter you will learn about arranging music to help avoid this. The point to remember now is that you should only downshift when you want to create an atmosphere of peace, serenity, focus, or quiet. Consider this popular worship chorus:

"Think about His Love"
  Verse 1 in key of C "Think about his love . . ."
  Verse 2 in key of B♭ "Think about his love . . ." (ever so slightly
           slower, softer. . .)

The difference between modulating and staying in one key for verse after verse is like the difference between color versus black and white on TV. Let's learn how.

Modulating

There's a Weak Way and a Bunch of Right Ways

Imagine your congregation loves to sing "Lord I Lift Your Name on High" over and over. You determine that since this song is about "lifting" and uses the word "high," it might work well to modulate to a higher key between the second and third time you play through it. The *weaker way* would be to finish verse 2, then immediately slam into the new key. This would likely jolt the congregation, several people would continue singing it in the old key (how embarrassing), and it would simply feel awkward.

The Secret Is Transition Chords

To make your modulations really work, you need to play one or more chords *between* the old key and the new key. These are your transition chords. They work like audio punctuation marks, automatically, subliminally telling your listeners that something different is about to happen. Transition chords are the bridges that connect one key to another. If you listen to praise and worship recordings, you will hear these transition chords all over the place whether you realize it or not.

Your Formula for Success

The good news is all you have to do to create transition chords is follow a formula. In the section that follows you will learn and try several of these formulas, which all work remarkably well. In fact, they work all the time, without fail between any two keys! Which ones will make their way into your playing? They are all based on a similar formula, but each one has a subtle tonal difference. Let your ears be the judge. We have suggested certain ones for different occasions, but don't be bound by our suggestions.

What you *will* need to know in advance is what the two keys are that you will be moving between. In the modulation methods we will use the example of moving between C and D, but the formulas will work between any two keys. These usually work well, but as always in real life, let your ears be your guide.

To help you with your modulations, we have listed transition chords in two ways. First, we will present the intervals for those of you who understand them. If you don't know what an interval is, relax; following the intervals is a plain language chart that literally shows you exactly what to play. In this chapter the methods are explained, and in the appendix, you'll find a ready-reference transition chord finder for the most popular keys.

Modulation Method 1

When you are in a fast moving song, perhaps the best way to modulate is to finish the last measure of the song in the first key, then play the dominant seventh of the fifth of the new key for either one measure or, if you're in a hurry, at the end of the measure, then jump right into the new key. The intervals would look like this:

Old key	Transition chord (in new key)	New key
I (root)	V7 (dominant 7th of the new key, play for 1 measure)	I (root)

Example: Modulating from C to D

Old key	Transition chord (in new key)	New key
C (root)	A7 (dominant 7th of the new key, play for 1 measure)	D (root)
[G, C, E]	[G, A, C#, E]	[F#, A, D]

Modulation Method 2

Here is another popular and easy modulation method that works well for moderate tempo songs. Like method 1, finish the last measure of the song in the first key. Then play the fourth of the new key for half a measure, then the dominant seventh of the fifth of the new key for half a measure, then jump right into the new key. The intervals would look like this:

Old key	Transition chord (in new key)	Transition chord (in new key)	New key
I (root)	IV (2 beats)	V7 (2 beats)	I (root)

Example: Modulating from C to D

Old key	Transition chord (in new key)	Transition chord (in new key)	New key
C (root)	G (2 beats)	A7 (2 beats)	D (root)
[G, C, E]	[G, B, D]	[G, A, C#, E]	[F#, A, D]

Modulation Method 3

This method uses a minor 7th chord for one of the transition chords. We like this modulation method for songs in the 6/8 time signature. Like the other methods, start by finishing the last measure of the song in the first key. Then play the minor second dominant seventh of the new key for a full measure, then the dominant seventh of the fifth of the new key for a full measure, then jump right into the new key. In a 6/8 time signature, the intervals would look like this:

Old key	Transition chord (in new key)	Transition chord (in new key)	New key
I (root)	ii7 (1 measure)	V7 (1 measure)	I (root)

Example: Modulating from C to D

Old key	Transition chord (in new key)	Transition chord (in new key)	New key
C (root)	Em7 (6 beats)	A7 (6 beats)	D (root)
[G, C, E]	[G, B, D, E]	[G, A, C#, E]	[F#, A, D]

Modulation Method 4

This method is similar to the last one but it ends with the gorgeous 11th chord. This is a favorite modulation method for slow songs and ballads. Like the other methods, start by finishing the last measure of the song in the first key. Then play the minor second 7th of the new key for a full measure, then the 11th of the fifth of the new key for a full measure, then slide right into the new key. The intervals would look like this:

Old key	Transition chord (in new key)	Transition chord (in new key)	New key
I (root)	ii7 (1 measure)	IV/V (1 measure)	I (root)

Example: Modulating from C to D

Old key	Transition (in new key)	Transition (in new key)	New key
C (root)	Em7 (1 measure)	G/A (1 measure)	D (root)
[G, C, E]	[G, B, D, E]	[G, B, D, with A in the bass]	[F#, A, D]

Modulation Method 5

This final method is known as the *shazaam*. In other circles, it is the *fat daddy*. When you need to be dramatic, use this one. It is similar to the previous examples, but it incorporates an inversion of the magical "13 flatted 9" chord, the formula for which is (LH—root) 5, 13, dom7, ♭9, 3. Confused? Take a look:

C13♭9 = (LH) C (RH) G, A, B♭, D♭, E

Like the other methods, start by finishing the last measure of the song in the first key. Then play the minor second 7th of the new key for a full measure, then the 13♭9 of the perfect 5th of the new key for a full measure. This time, hold that chord for the whole measure to let it sink in. Then slide into the new key. The intervals would look like this:

Old key	Transition chords (in new key)	Transition (in new key)	New key
I (root)	ii7 (1 measure)	V13♭9 (1 measure)	I (root)

Example: Modulating from E♭ to F

Old key	Transition chords (in new key)	Transition chords (in new key)	New key
E♭ (root)	Gm7 (1 measure)	C13♭9 (1 measure)	F (root)
[G, B♭, E♭]	[G, B♭, D, F]	[G, A, B♭, D♭, E with C in the bass]	[F, A, C]

If you don't understand intervals, there is an easy-to-use chart with all the keys included in the appendix of this book.

Learn to Transpose on the Spot

The best musicians can transpose spontaneously. They don't even have to think about it. To them, modulation is as natural as breathing.

For the rest of us, this skill comes only with a great deal of practice. However, if you play by reading chord symbols, there are two things you can do to get started. First, you can quickly modulate up a whole step by learning to think alphabetically.

Let's say your first song is in the key of C. As you read the chord symbols . . . C . . . F . . . D . . . G . . . you can think to yourself, *Hmmm, if I want to modulate up a whole step I just need to step up a whole letter in the alphabet.*

So in this song, C becomes D, F becomes G, D becomes E, and G becomes A (since there's no H in music).

That's spontaneous transposition! The bad thing about this method is it doesn't *always* work! For example, although F follows E in the alphabet, when transposing up a whole step, E becomes F♯, not F-natural. This is because of the way the chromatic scale is organized. Thinking alphabetically is still a good method because if you are modulating and a chord sounds really rotten, the fix usually comes when you slide up one note on the keyboard or one fret on the guitar. Though it is not a perfect method, it works most of the time.

The second thing you can do to spontaneously transpose is to cheat. You'll learn to do this in chapter 2 by simply writing the new chord symbols right on your music sheets.

Technology Can Help with the Full Piano Score or Printed Music

If you can't read chord symbols and you absolutely must have printed music, you can get computer scoring/notation software to do the transposition and modulation work for you. We won't go into much detail here; we will simply explain how it works.

First, you plug a MIDI-compatible keyboard into your computer using a special interface. Next you start the software and play the music into your computer, which records it into memory. Then you click a button and sheet music magically appears on your screen. "Big deal," you say. "I already had the music." Here's where the magic happens.

Next you click another button, choose a new key, and the music is instantly (and perfectly) transposed on screen. Click "print" and you have instant sheet music! The process takes a little getting used to, but if you require printed music or work with an orchestra and need to produce music for horn and reed instruments, scoring/notation software is indispensable.

Sneaky Embellishments to Colorize Your Playing

Embellishments are the fancy little ditties that make your music interesting. Learning new embellishments is a lot like playing tennis. The best way to improve is to get around someone better than you and ask them to give you some pointers.

There are literally hundreds of things you can do to make your playing more interesting. In the classified ads of music magazines there are often plenty of ads for books, cassettes, videos, and CDs that promise to teach you how to play in certain styles. If you are comfortable using the Internet, type "piano style" or "guitar lessons" into your search engine and you'll be amazed at what turns up.

Fortunately, we have bought many of these products, and we are happy to report that with a few exceptions, most are pretty good. We recommend you have a look. Before you do though, let us give you a few embellishments to try out.

When Not to Embellish

One of the first things you need to understand is when and when not to embellish. First, embellishments should never be done for their own sake. Ostentatious gimmicks don't lend themselves well to worship music. Second, avoid embellishing during a lyric phrase. You don't want the instruments to compete with the lyrics.

Finally, you don't want two or more instruments to freestyle at the same time (unless perhaps they are in unison). Two instruments competing sounds horrible. We remember one church where there was an "orchestra." It seemed that in every section there was a prima donna of sorts. During the music, at the end of almost every phrase, a trumpet would trail off in one direction, a flute in another, the drummer would roll, and the violin would vibrato off into the sunset. It was awful.

Embellish the Right Way

Usually, you will want to embellish at the end of a phrase, when the singers are holding a half note or longer. Study the following examples.

$^3/_4$ | There is no | shadow of | turning with | Thee . . .

[embellish here]

While the singers are holding the word "Thee," *one* of the instruments can freestyle for beats 2 and 3 of the measure.

Here are three easy methods to embellishing.

Method 1
Change chord inversions up on $^1/_4$ notes.

Beat 1   Beat 2   Beat 3   Beat 4
CEG/C EGC/C GCE/C CEG/C (These are played as chords on the quarter beat.)

Method 2
Run chord notes up or down on 8th notes.

Beat 1   Beat 2   Beat 3   Beat 4
CE/C   GC/C   EG/C   CE/C   (These are played as individual notes on the eighth beat.)

Method 3
Open chord (remove middle note) move down on quarters.

Beat 1   Beat 2   Beat 3   Beat 4
GC/C   EG/C   CE/C   CG/C   (These are played as chords on the quarter beat.)

QUICK TIPS: DO'S and DON'ts FOR PLaYeRS

In this section you will find a number of musical ideas and skill-building strategies. Many of you will feel like a kid in a candy store, eagerly filling your pockets with every conceivable musical confection. Like that kid you will want to try each and every one as soon as possible. You need to avoid this temptation.

On the other hand, some of you might resist trying anything new that requires effort and getting used to. Avoiding this temptation is even more important than the first one. Taking the easy road and staying with the familiar is, well, easy. Any skilled musician will tell you they regularly push themselves beyond their comfort zone to grow and stay fresh. Do some of the stuff in this section and we promise little by little your playing will change—for the better.

Listen to Talented Musicians in Other Musical Genres

Being primarily a keyboard player, I (Doug) love to listen to jazz pianists—the really good ones. For elegance and incredibly textured chord voicing, there's Joe Sample. For sheer virtuosity there's Chick Corea. I could listen to jazz all day. But that would be indulgence. Since I don't play much jazz in church (although I regularly sneak stuff in), I need to listen to other styles, including (gulp!) country.

As you listen, listen selectively. Don't just enjoy the song; go deeper into the music. Single out and listen for *your* instrument's part and analyze it.

When I (Tami) listen to a bassist, I try to figure out several things: What is the bassist doing—picking, plucking, or slapping? What register is the bassist playing in—low, mid, or high? Is the bassist playing lots of notes or just a few? Does the bassist play mostly the root note of the chord or does she use a lot of passing notes? Then, I'll try to mimic what they do. It works really well.

Keyboardists: Don't Play Hymnal Style

If you are the type of player who stays glued to the printed music, unfortunately you are at a distinct disadvantage if you want a big contemporary sound. Here's why: Hymnals (and far too many praise and worship songbooks) score or print music according to four parts.

What you see on the page is not the keyboard part, but rather the vocal parts. Pianists and organists who have grown up musically in the church have learned to play simply what is written, i.e., the vocal score. The result is that the singers and keys do exactly the same thing. This dual sound is sometimes called playing *hymnal style* or *block chords.*

The problem with this is that the keyboardists on your favorite praise and worship recordings almost never play block chords. They play their own part. In fact, you will be hard pressed to find modern professional keyboardists playing adult contemporary music in hymnal style.

Now, you might justifiably ask, *How in the world am I supposed to play a part that's not written in the music?*

The answer is . . . you fake it.

One of the things you need to unlearn when playing modern praise and worship music is simply playing the four parts written in the music. If you do that, *you're overplaying.* Here are two suggestions to help you fix it:

First, try playing fewer notes. Especially on moderate and slow ballads, try to just hold the first chord of a measure (as long as it sounds right) without playing the melody. Your goal is to let the singers carry the melody. For your left hand, play the root of the chord an octave apart.

Second, observe the chord symbols above the melody line to see where to lift and strike a new chord. Chances are, your ears will also "tell" you when to change and hold a new chord.

Guitarists: Get the Right Kind of Capo

If you *must* use a capo, by all means get the right kind. There are several kinds of capos for guitarists. By far the worst is the elastic, rubber band type. If you have one of these in your guitar case, put this book down right now and go throw it away. These wretched examples of poor engineering always require two hands to install, requiring you to stop everything and wrestle them into place.

The best and, therefore, only choice for you is the "pincher" type. These capos lock on to your guitar in a fraction of a second and, best of all, can be installed with just one hand. Also, you can place it on the head of your guitar when it's not in use. To install one during a song, learn how to hold your chord with your left hand, then reach around with your right to grab and install the capo.

If you need to change keys and yet insist on playing the same set of chords, you can do it with one of these and not miss a beat. Sure, they cost more, but they're worth it.

Don't Ever Go Onstage without Tuning Up

Always. Always. Always tune up before ministering. Only the sound of a cat stuck in a chimney is worse than instruments out of tune. Okay, that's probably an overstatement. The fact is, once you start playing an out-of-tune instrument, there's no smooth way to correct it. You will distract people's worship experience one way or another. Always tune up.

Guitarists: Have You Tried a Twelve-String Guitar?

If you are the kind of guitarist who does a lot of chord strumming, consider getting a twelve-string guitar. The feel of a twelve-string is noticeably different—it tends to feel a little bulky at first, but the sound of a twelve-string is enormous!

Thick, lush, and rich sounding, a twelve-string might be just what you need to create a spaciousness to your sound. If you are considering purchasing a twelve-string, choose carefully. Get to a music store that has more than one or two twelve-strings and play every single one in the store until you find the one that feels best—then buy it. Forget about things like colors and focus instead on what we call the action. When it comes to guitars, "action" refers to the distance between the strings and the frets.

Here's another secret many twelve-string players use: Installing light or even extra light strings can make a big difference in making the instrument easier to play. Don't worry about losing volume; your amplifier will make up the difference. By the way, if you can get your hands on an electric twelve-string, consider yourself doubly blessed. (No pun intended!) The sound of these babies is absolutely incredible.

Check with Other Players Before You Substitute Chords

This is a big mistake garage-band players make all the time. Substituting chords is usually a terrific idea, as long as everyone knows what's going on. Many of the chord substitutions in this chapter sound fine when played on top of simple triads; however, the different substitutions rarely sound good played on top of each other. For example, if you play an Em9, it will be fine if your other players play an Em, but you don't want them playing Em7♭5.

A most common substitution faux pas is suspending chords. Guitarists are notorious for suspending the 4th of the D chord. This is fine *only* when everyone suspends. If the keyboards stay on D while the guitars suspend, you'll get dissonant slop. Remember, always ask first.

Guitarists: Electric and Acoustic Guitars Are Played Differently

It makes us cringe every time we hear it. Someone buys an electric (solid body) guitar, then gets up on the platform and strums it wildly as if it were an acoustic.

Now we understand there might be some disagreement here. After all, there are literally dozens of musical styles. To be sure, for some musical styles, the guitar part could be played on both electric and/or acoustic.

However, when it comes to the adult contemporary sound popular in today's praise and worship music, you should think of electric and acoustic guitars as different instruments, with different roles and different playing styles. We like to compare it to the difference between playing piano and organ. While both have keyboards and the fundamentals are the same, there are distinctive differences in the way each is played.

We can't devote much space here on distinguishing the differences, but we can warn you with this: Few professionals aggressively strum an electric guitar while playing basic chords on the first three frets. The electric guitar part on today's adult contemporary music uses unique chords and picking styles. Basically, when you make the transition from acoustic to electric guitar, you will need to develop a lighter touch. Don't aggressively strum them like acoustic guitars. Just don't.

If you want to be an electric guitarist, learn the basics on your acoustic folk guitar, then build your alternate, electric technique with some private lessons.

in CLOSING

Congratulations! You have covered plenty of ground in this chapter. Before you move on, there is one final assignment: Keeping your finger in this spot, glance back through this chapter and write yourself a reminder of several things you most want to apply. Do it right now, so you don't forget.

Things I Need to Apply from This Chapter:

1. _____ (page _____)
2. _____ (page _____)
3. _____ (page _____)
4. _____ (page _____)
5. _____ (page _____)

chapter 2

Give Your Arrangements a Tune-up

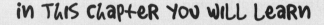

in This Chapter You Will Learn

- How to design a playlist that creates a focused worship experience.
- How to prepare music and charts for your worship team.
- What you need to know about copyright issues.
- How to arrange with dynamics and mixed instruments.
- How to arrange with transitions and segues to get a seamless flow.
- Quick tips: do's and don'ts for arranging worship music.

introduction to This Chapter

Chances are, you have attended worship services where there was a wonderful atmosphere. As you worshiped in spirit and in truth, you were carried along effortlessly, like a Frisbee in the wind, as the music lifted you to new heights. Chances are you have also attended worship services where the opposite was true. The service (especially the music) felt artificial, wooden, choppy, and erratic. Perhaps you felt as if the worship was punctuated by abrupt starts, stops, and rambling soliloquies that felt contrived and weak.

What makes the difference? Certainly there are spiritual factors at play in each situation. We in no way want to diminish the importance of the character and attitude of those who lead worship. However, we would like to suggest that the atmosphere, the feeling in the air of a worship service, can be carefully and intentionally created. That's right—it is the result of careful planning. It happens because someone skillfully arranged the music and "flow" for the worship service.

Do you admire the "professional" contemporary praise and worship leaders you hear on recordings? Of course you do. Now hear this. Although it might *sound* as if everything is happening spontaneously on these recordings, that's rarely the case. More often than not (and there are exceptions), the music, transitions, and arrangements are carefully and systematically designed to lead or guide the congregation through a variety of emotions and experiences.

God Uses Careful Planning

Please don't misunderstand. We're not in any way downplaying the need for Spirit-filled leadership.

What we are suggesting, though, is that God clearly seems to work *through* planning and arranging. It's not *either* Spirit-filled leadership *or* intentional planning. It's both. Perhaps that's one of the reasons we are told God wants church worship services done "in a fitting and orderly way" (1 Corinthians 14:40).

GOD WORKS through CAREFUL PLANNING.

If you want to lead life-changing worship services, you'll need to do much more than simply string a bunch of songs together. You will need to skillfully arrange them. Some worship leaders who plan services seem to have a natural gift for this and are able to do it almost without thinking about it. For the rest of us, it is a discipline that must be learned. Fortunately for you, that's what this chapter is about.

When It Comes to Arranging, You Have Three Tasks

Every week you have to create a playlist. Whether you realize it or not, this is a threefold task.

1. You need to *pick your songs*. Throughout the rest of this book, the group or set of songs you use during a given worship service will be referred to as a "playlist." Once you establish your playlist, you are ready for step two.

2. You must *get the music* in the playlist ready for everyone on your worship team. Choir directors know all about pulling music and loading choir folders week in, week out. Most praise and worship teams are nowhere near this organized! Instead, their music collection is a hodgepodge of handwritten chord charts, photocopied music, and well-worn songbooks. There are a number of things you need to know about when pulling your music together for your team, which you will find in this chapter.

3. Finally, you will want to decide how you'll *arrange the songs* in your playlist. Hopefully, you won't operate like a junior high garage band—everybody playing and singing all at once, all the time. It's much more professional to skillfully blend instruments and voices in and out, combine some of the songs together into medleys, provide a spoken introduction here and there, build in an occasional key change, etc.

While some leaders like to plan and arrange on the fly during rehearsals, we hope you will at least consider trying to arrange more deliberately in advance.

In this chapter we will look closely at each of the above three tasks and try to provide you with ideas and examples that will help you approach each in a purposeful way. Like other chapters in this book, you might not ultimately apply everything you read about here. Hopefully though, a few ideas and concepts will challenge you to further refine your skills as a worship leader.

> GET BEYOND the "EVERYBODY-PLAYING-AT-ONCE-ALL-THE-TIME" METHOD OF ARRANGING!

how to Design a Playlist That Creates a Focused Worship experience

How do you design a playlist? First, let's look at the wrong way:

- Grab a songbook or hymnal and start flipping through the pages. *Oh, that song looks good.*
- Flip a few more pages. *The congregation always likes that one.*
- Flip. Flip. Flip. *That one has a cool bass part! Let's do that one again.*
- And so on.

While flipping through songbooks might be a valid way to get ideas, we are convinced there's a better way: creating a playlist on purpose. In other words, rather than choosing songs for your playlist arbitrarily, you deliberately choose songs to accomplish a specific goal.

Why do you choose one song over another? Some worship leaders choose songs by their appeal: *The congregation likes this one!* Others look for themes: *The pastor is speaking on giving, so let's pick a song about. . . .* These are fine as far as they go, but if you want to design even more life-changing worship experiences, you will need to go deeper. In the sections that follow, we want to offer a three-tiered model that will help you do just that.

Arranging for a Meaningful Worship Experience

Tier 3

Direct attention of worship in a specific direction.

Song direction

Tier 2

Focus the congregation's thoughts on a theme.

Song content

Tier 1

Carefully select tempos to control the feel in the room.

Atmosphere

Tier 1: Arranging Music to Create an Atmosphere

For just a moment, forget about song theme, song lyrics, and congregational response. Think back to the types of worship services we mentioned at the beginning of this chapter. Try to remember a service you attended where there was a tremendous sense of continuity, spiritual flow, and feeling of corporate oneness. Hopefully, you have been in services where you effortlessly drifted from hand-clapping, heart-pounding, joyous enthusiasm to a sense of quiet, contemplative awe at the throne of God. Don't you just love services where you seamlessly migrate from mood to mood, emotion to emotion, laughter to tears, enjoying the process without noticing the transitions? You leave such services feeling refreshed in your spirit, invigorated, and closer to Christ.

We firmly believe it is the Holy Spirit who stirs our hearts. However, we have also observed that he seems to do this more often when worship, *especially the music and art forms,* are carefully planned. It seems that the best worship services—those where people truly sense they have entered the presence of God, respond personally to him, and experience genuine edification—are those where someone, usually the worship leader, has put some time and thought into the service. Our belief is that God rewards hard work and planning and that he carefully guides worship leaders who invest time and effort in their planning and arrangements.

Your First Job Is to "Set the Room," or Create an Atmosphere

The first thing you should think about when planning a service is not the lyrics, or sermon theme, but on the way you want the room to "feel" at various places in the service. There are times when you want your congregation to move into a contemplative, meditative, more serious mood. At other times you want them celebrating. There are also times when you might want them to go into a cognitive, or "thinking" mode. How do you do this? You use your music. Let's start by introducing the relationship between music and human emotions.

Like It or Not, Your Playlists Will Create Emotions

This might seem radical to some readers, but we believe music, the actual notes you play and the way you play them—yes, the very sounds themselves—can profoundly influence the way people feel. Are we saying musical sounds can actually change the way people feel? Yes—especially for those who are willing to be changed.

Musicologists are people who study the science of music. One of the facets of this field is the effect of music on human behavior and emotions. From their work, we know that music has the capacity to influence human emotion. While we don't have time to offer a detailed exposition on this phenomenon, consider these examples.

At slow tempos, most people think minor chords sound "sadder," or "more thoughtful" than major chords.

At fast tempos, 7th chords sound "happier" or "brighter" than major chords. Many people identify 7th chords with a flatted 5th as "sarcastic sounding."

Want to write a romantic love song? The keys of E♭ and A♭ sound more "romantic" than other keys to most people.

Want to scare people or make them nervous? The perfect tritone interval is identified with the demonic or devilish. In fact, one rumor suggests this musical interval was banned in some medieval churches! Curious? Play a series of quarter notes alternating between middle C and F♯.

Repetitive rhythms make it much easier for people to drift into trance-like or altered states of consciousness.

As an art form, music has a powerful emotional effect on people. As a worship leader, you can try to understand and leverage this knowledge, or you can ignore it and approach your task haphazardly. The choice is up to you. We will assume you want to understand music and use it for good! Let's look now at musical structure.

Understanding Musical Structure

Most modern Western music, including contemporary praise and worship music, is structured in a pretty predictable manner.

1. First, there's a verse.
2. After the verse, there's a chorus.
3. Then there's a second verse that uses the same melody of the first verse, but with different lyrics.
4. Then the chorus is repeated . . . and so on.

Some people call this musical structure the "A/B format." In other words, the verse is the A part, followed by the chorus, or B part. Most praise and worship music and many of the hymns you sing at church follow this structure: A/B/A/B and so on. There's nothing wrong with this, but let's face it: it's not too interesting.

If It's Not Baroque, Don't Fix It

If you examine music written during the Baroque period (e.g., Bach), you will notice that the music is structured differently. Instead of using the predictable A/B/A/B structure, composers during the Baroque period had a different agenda. They wanted their music to move people through a series of emotions.

That's why their music was written according to dispositions, or "attitudes." Consider the structure of a concerto from Bach's Brandenburg Concertos:

Allegro
Andante
Presto

Now, if you were able to sit down with J. S. Bach and ask him what he meant by these instructional words, he would likely say something like this:

When you perform part 1, the Allegro, play it light and bouncy. I want people to feel bright and fresh, like it's the first day of spring! When you get to part 2, the Andante, change everything. Shift the listener's mood. Make them feel more somber and serious, but retain a sense of lilt.

When you get to part 3, the Presto, play it fast! Return the listener to a feeling of brightness, hope, and joy!

Baroque music was often evaluated by its ability to move people from mood to mood. If a composer's music moved people skillfully, it was praised. If it lacked the ability to do so, it was scorned. Attending a Baroque concert was supposed to be an experience where the listener was moved by the music through a wide range of human emotions. The composers of the Baroque period not only knew music could be used to shift people's emotions, they were masters at doing so. We need to learn from them.

It's in the Bible Too

Not convinced? Biblical music contains the same kind of thing. Although we don't know exactly what the music of David sounded like, we do know that the way the music was played was important to the musicians of his day. The musicians and worship leaders who played the psalms in the temple wanted them to be played a certain way—to create a certain feeling. In fact, they even supplied playing instructions with many of the psalms in your Bible.

Often ignored by Bible readers, many psalms contain what biblical scholars call superscriptions. Superscriptions are words and phrases contained at the beginning of a psalm that provide not just historical information but also musical instructions for players, singers, and leaders. Here are a few examples:

Maskil: A psalm to be used for teaching (cf. Ps. 32; 42; 44; 45; 52).

Selah: A musical term probably meaning "instruments only." Most scholars think this meant people were to stop singing and think about the preceding lyrics while an instrument played a solo (cf. Ps. 20; 24; 32; 47; et. al).

Neginath: Probably means "Play this psalm with stringed instruments" (Ps. 4; 54; 61).

Nehiloth: Probably means "Play this psalm with wind instruments" (Ps. 5).

Muth-Labban: Probably means "Play it slow, like a funeral song" (Ps. 9).

Alamoth: Probably means "The young women should sing this song" (Ps. 46).

What's Your Point?

Biblical musicians and Baroque composers knew music could steer people's moods. As a worship leader, you need to carefully plan to use music in the same way. Part of your role as a worship leader is to skillfully use music to steer people's minds and emotions toward worship. We believe God wants *you* to get behind the wheel and drive! In other words, if you're called to be a leader, *lead!*

Arranging with Tempo and Feel

Take tempo for example. While it might seem like common sense, make sure that when you arrange songs, you avoid dramatic shifts in tempo. In other words, if you want people to feel like celebrating, to be happy and joyous, don't play fast and slow songs right next to each other. Keep the tempo up on all the songs until you want the atmosphere and people's emotions to change.

Professional musicians traditionally use Italian words to describe tempo and feel. For our arranging purposes, though, we will divide popular praise and worship music into four broad tempo families. If you are new to identifying tempo, get a metronome (or use the drum machine in your keyboard) and train your ears to identify tempos.

Each tempo family tends to be useful for designing a different type of atmosphere—a feel in the room. If you want to be a skillful worship leader, learn these tempo families and use them intelligently and deliberately.

As you examine the following four tempo families, sing through each song example and sense how the tempo makes you feel. Ask yourself: *Do I agree with the type of atmosphere each family is best suited for?* How might you use this knowledge in your worship services?

Tempo Family #1: Slow Ballad

Tempo range: 60–80 bpm (beats per minute)

Use songs in this tempo family when you want the atmosphere to be:

> Meditative
> Tranquil
> Easy to listen to God's voice
> Contemplative
> Full of promise
> Serene
> Calming
> Gently encouraging
> Winding down

Hymnal examples:

> "O Sacred Head, Now Wounded"
> "Just As I Am"
> "Near to the Heart of God"
> "I Surrender All"

Chorus examples:
    "Praise the Name of Jesus"
    "I Stand in Awe"
    "As the Deer"
    "Think about His Love"
    "I Love You, Lord"
    "More Precious Than Silver"

Tempo Family #2: Moderate Ballad
Tempo range: 80–100 bpm

Use songs in this tempo family when you want the atmosphere to be:
    Focusing on truth
    Challenging
    Enjoining, motivating
    Regal, royal
    Robust
    Courageous
    Cognitive
    Confident
    Solid, firm

Hymnal examples:
    "Immortal, Invisible, God Only Wise"
    "All Creatures of Our God and King"
    "Reach Out to Jesus"

Chorus examples:
    "Shout to the Lord"
    "Majesty"
    "All Hail King Jesus"
    "Open the Eyes of My Heart"
    "Shine, Jesus, Shine"
    "I Sing Praises to Your Name"
    "I Could Sing of Your Love Forever"

Tempo Family #3: Light Pop
Tempo Range: 100–120 bpm

Use songs in this tempo family when you want the atmosphere to be:

Warm, friendly
Sociable
Upbeat but not rowdy
Enthusiastic
Testimonial
Happy, relaxed
Easy to clap to
Foot-tapping
Welcoming, cheerful

Hymnal examples:
"Christ the Lord Is Risen Today"
"Our Great Savior"
"At Calvary"
"Wonderful Grace of Jesus"

Chorus examples:
"We Bring the Sacrifice of Praise"
"Lord, I Lift Your Name on High"
"This Is the Day"
"We Believe"
"Because He Lives"
"Something Beautiful"
"I Will Call upon the Lord"
"O Happy Day"

Tempo Family #4: Fast Pop
Tempo: 120–160 bpm

Use songs in this tempo family when you want the atmosphere to be:
Joyful
Motivational
Stimulating
Celebratory
Fired up
Energetic
Charged

Hymn examples:
"Since Jesus Came into My Heart"
"I'll Fly Away"
"In My Heart There Rings a Melody"

Chorus examples:
"Great and Mighty is the Lord Our God"
"Celebrate Jesus"
"Making War in the Heavenlies"
"He Is Exalted"
"Jehovah Jireh"

What to Make of the Four Tempo Families

As you construct your playlist, keeping the songs clustered by tempo family will help your congregation stay focused and in the groove. Mixing songs from different tempo families in close proximity to one another does the opposite—it makes the service feel choppy and disjointed.

Envision your worship service the way the Baroque composers approached their concerts. Your goal is to move people through a series of experiences. Like the composers of sixteenth century, you will carefully choose your tempo, lyric content theme, and audience focus to deliberately direct people's minds and emotions. You will skillfully guide your people through worship-inspiring ideas and sounds.

Depending on the amount of time your church typically dedicates to the praise and worship team, you might like to plan your movements like the great composers—in clearly delineated segments, with smooth transitions.

Tier 2: Focusing the Congregation's Thoughts on a Theme

Once you have determined to focus the congregation's emotions, you are ready for the next tier: their thoughts. Let's stop here for just a moment. Have you ever listened to a sermon, then after the service asked yourself, *What was that message about?* and came up empty? The minister may have said lots of good things, cracked a few funny jokes, and said things that you agreed with, but if someone asked you to summarize the main point of the message in one sentence, you couldn't. In fact, you doubt the pastor could. Unfortunately, many teachers, public speakers, and ministers present good content in a haphazard, undisciplined, unfocused way. One of the fundamental truths of great public speaking and solid instructional design is that people engage with content better when it is focused around and built upon clear learning objectives, propositional statements, and central ideas. In other words, world-class public speakers, teachers, and preachers figure out exactly what content they want their audience to engage with, then they develop and present their content to hit that target.

What does this mean to you as you arrange your worship service? It means you should do the same thing. Instead of choosing songs in a borderline arbitrary fashion, put some more thought into it. Here's how.

Ask a Question—Then Answer It

Start by thinking about the big picture of your worship service. Ask yourself this important question: *What do I want to happen during worship?*

Your answer must go well beyond a general, superficial response like "Worship!" Force yourself to drill down. Get specific. Focus. Perhaps a better way to ask it is: *What do I want people to think about during this part of the worship service?*

Ask God to guide you toward a specific answer. Part of your role as a worship leader is to lead or to steer. This means you direct people toward specific ideas that promote worship.

Here are a few examples (both good and not so good) to get you started.

Less than ideal:

    God
    Jesus
    Praise
    The church

These are good concepts, but as specific ideas to promote worship, they are far too general. What about God? What about Jesus? Why praise? What about the church?

Now, consider the following ideas:

    God is majestic and powerful.
    Jesus forgives me even though I fail.
    I will praise God because of the wonderful things he has done in my life.
    It's good to come to church and be with God's people.

With clear, specific ideas like these, you can quickly build a focused playlist resulting in a focused congregational worship experience. Your motive is to focus your people on a specific idea like those listed above.

Your goal is to come up with a theme for worship. Some worship leaders ask their pastor to give them a one-sentence summary of their upcoming sermon, then use that as their theme. However you come up with it, make it a clear, propositional statement.

By the way, there is nothing wrong with having several themes or ideas around which to build your playlist. For example, if you minister in a church with a lengthy worship time, you might want to lead the people in worship through a series of ideas, like this:

> Jesus watches over his children.
> God can be trusted, even when life hurts.
> God can bring good things out of bad experiences.
> God is big and powerful.

Notice in the above set of themes a clear progression of concepts. It almost looks like the outline of a sermon doesn't it? In fact, if you can pull off this sort of thing, you will be leading your people in a sort of sermon in song. That's awesome!

Once you have chosen the idea or ideas you want your people to think about, you will be ready to start choosing songs that support your theme(s).

Let's Get Analytical

Now it is time to start brainstorming or, if you must, flipping through song-books and hymnals! Get a piece of paper and write down as many songs that relate to your worship theme as you can think of. In the appendix of this book there is a Song Screening Worksheet you might find helpful.

Many hymnals and chorus books contain topical indexes. Major headings, such as Lordship, God the Father, or Communion, are followed by a list of hymns and songs to choose from. These indexes are treasure troves you should become comfortable with. Often you can put together extremely effective playlists quickly by comparing the indexes from several hymnals and chorus books, then drawing songs from each.

hint: Learn to use topical indexes to locate theme music.

Tier 3: Focus the Congregation's Attention

Now, look at your preliminary list of songs and ask this important question about each song: *Who are we singing to?*

Some praise and worship songs are directed at God, while others are directed at people. Some songs are introspective and function as personal reminders to oneself. When you begin trimming your list you can probably divide the music into several categories.

Songs Asking God to Do Something

These songs are in effect "sung prayers." Take a moment and sing through a few bars of each of the following popular praise and worship choruses and you will see each one is addressed *to* God, and in each we *ask* God to do something.

"Change My Heart O God"
"Savior, Like a Shepherd Lead Us"
"Glorify Thy Name"
"Open Our Eyes, Lord"
"In My Life, Lord, Be Glorified"

Songs Offering Praise, Giving Thanks, Making Statements to God

Other songs don't ask anything of God, but rather make statements *to* him, often affirming truth, giving adoration, and ascribing greatness. Sing through a few bars of the following and you will see what we mean.

"Holy, Holy, Holy"
"Lord, I Lift Your Name on High"
"As the Deer"
"I Love You, Lord"
"We Bow Down"

As you sang each of the above pieces, you didn't ask anything of God, did you? You made statements *to* him though. That's the difference.

Songs Directed At Others or Ourselves

Finally, there are many songs of admonition, in which we encourage others (or ourselves) to do or say something. These have been called "testimony songs" in some circles because they are meant to help others. Consider the following examples. Each one makes a declarative statement not to God, but to people.

"Awesome God"
"Celebrate Jesus"
"Give Thanks"
"Seek Ye First"
"Isn't He?"
"Because He Lives"
"God Will Make a Way"
"Majesty"
"Praise the Name of Jesus"

Cluster Songs According to Intended Focus

One effective way to instantly give your worship services a much better sense of flow and continuity is to group songs according to their intended focus. Firmly decide what the song is designed to do:

- Ask something of God?
- Say something to God?
- Say something to other people?

This is another way to purposefully focus the congregation's attention. For example, sing two songs back to back where God is thanked for his goodness, then segue to a couple of songs where you encourage others to respond to God based on what you just sang about.

"How Great Thou Art" (Sung to God)
"Almighty, Most Glorious Lord" (Sung to God)

Spoken segue: "Let's continue thinking about God's mighty power. . . ."

"Mighty Is Our God" (Sung to other people)
"Blessed Be the Name of the Lord" (Sung to other people)

Let's wrap up this section by again reviewing the chart we started with. You've learned that you can create a meaningful playlist and worship experience by building your music on a three-tiered model:

ARRANGING FOR A MEANINGFUL WORSHIP EXPERIENCE

Tier 3

Direct attention of worship in a specific direction.

Song direction

Tier 2

Focus the congregation's thoughts on a theme.

Song content

Tier 1

Carefully select tempos to control the feel in the room.

Atmosphere

how to Prepare music and Charts for Your Worship Team

Once you have your preliminary playlist established, you need to ensure that everybody on your worship team has the same music. If you are like most worship leaders, there are four things about you that are true:

1. You pull music from a wide variety of sources.
2. Your photocopier cringes every time you enter the room with a songbook under your arm.
3. You run through reams of paper during the course of a year.
4. You have no intention of changing.

Unlike the choir directors mentioned earlier, few praise and worship teams keep songbooks and sheet music neatly organized. If you are going to use a stack of photocopied music, you need to know a few things about using it well and using it ethically.

How the Pros Prepare and Use Printed Music and Charts

Let's get four things straight: When it comes to using published music in the church, there are a few music publishing terms you need to understand and use correctly. Unfortunately, these terms are sometimes used interchangeably. To make sure you and your ministry stay legal, be sure you get them right.

Collections

Collections are individual printed pieces of music and/or songs bound together in book form. Your hymnal is a collection. The praise and music songbooks you use are collections. A book of piano offertories, the book your choir used for their last cantata, and the guitar book *The Best of Elvis* are all collections.

Octavos and Sheet Music

When you buy the printed music for just one song, it is called *sheet music.* Individual pieces of choral music are often called by their more traditional name: "octavo." (Octavos get their name because long ago they were eight pages in length. Today's octavos can be any number of pages, as long as they remain just one song.)

Chord Charts and Lead Sheets

Some people can't read printed music. They don't know the difference between a dotted eighth note and an accidental. Some people simply write or type the lyrics on a page, then place only the chord symbols above the lyrics. Whether the lyrics and chords are neatly typed with a computer or scribbled on the back of a napkin, if there are no staffs and notes, we call it a *chord chart*. Another closely related popular format used by many musicians is the *lead sheet*. Lead sheets contain lyrics, chord symbols, and a single staff with the melody.

Words-Only

The only thing that distinguishes a words-only piece from chord charts is the absence of the chord symbols. When we put just the lyrics (words) on an overhead transparency or print them in a bulletin, it's called *words-only*.

Which Way Should We Go?

So when it comes to your players and singers, which kind of music should you use? While everyone has a preference, most professionals would recommend using the printed music in collections and sheet music instead of chord charts for a few reasons.

1. **Notes.** Your vocalists (especially those who sing alto and bass) will need to see what notes to sing. While some singers who cover the nonmelody parts can "just hear it," you are likely to have at least one singer who thinks they can, but in reality everyone else in the band knows better. When you have printed music, there will be less arguing about what notes to sing.
2. **Timing.** When you have printed music, there's never a question of how many measures go between the end of the second chorus and the coda. Is that phrase sung with a series of eighth notes or is it dotted eighths followed by sixteenths? When you have the music, it will be right there in black and white.

The downside of using printed music is that the chord symbols supplied are often plain-Jane kindergarten chords. If you have worked through the material in this book in chapter 1, you will be scratching out the chords the publishers supply and inserting your own jazzy substitutions *(you sly dog)*.

Most praise and worship teams use a combination of both chord charts and printed music. However, when you reproduce and distribute music other people have written, be sure you don't violate copyright laws. (See page 61 for more information on copyright laws.)

Preparing Music for Your Worship Team

Let's get back to preparing music for your worship team. Assume you have your playlist, the songs are in order, and you are ready to start stuffing music into folders. Here are a few suggestions to keep in mind.

Enlarge Your Music

If everyone has their own copy of the songbooks you're using, you *can* make copies of the music on your photocopier. One of the benefits of this is the ability to enlarge the music to make it readable during performance. Experiment to get the music as big as you can. Look at the following diagram.

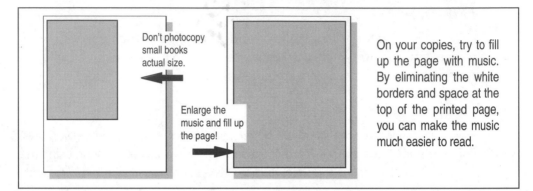

Don't photocopy small books actual size.

Enlarge the music and fill up the page!

On your copies, try to fill up the page with music. By eliminating the white borders and space at the top of the printed page, you can make the music much easier to read.

Don't Use Loose Sheets

Avoid using a stack of photocopied pages. Plenty of praise and worship team members have had the horrendously distracting experience of someone bumping into their music stand and scattering their music across the platform.

One way to keep your music organized is to use a three ring binder with vinyl sheet covers. Vinyl sheet covers are available at most business supply stores. You simply slip your photocopies right into the vinyl sheet covers. This is a great way to keep your music organized because your music won't get knocked off your stand as easily, you can easily arrange your music in performance order, and it is much easier to turn pages when you place them in the vinyl sheet covers.

There are different brands of vinyl sheet covers available. While all the vinyl covers are clear, some have a shiny finish while others have a matte finish. We prefer the less shiny types because they reflect less light, making them easier to read. Either type, however, will work.

Embellish Your Chord Charts, Lead Sheets, and Printed Music

There is another benefit to using vinyl sheet covers. If you use the type of felt tip pens designed for writing on overhead transparencies, you can easily mark up your chord charts without permanently altering them. Your writing is on the vinyl, not the paper. After the service, you just wipe it off.

This is especially useful if you want to write in the chord symbols for a key change. Some musicians like to write with a color other than black. That way, for example, the first time through they read the black chords, the second time through they read the red chords.

WHAT YOU NEED TO KNOW ABOUT COPYRIGHT ISSUES

We have been involved in music ministry for well over a decade, in many types of churches. Unfortunately, we have observed plenty of copyright violations. Whether it is done ignorantly, willfully, or naively, violating copyright law is always wrong.

Copyright Issues Then

At least in the United States, the old copyright law can be summed up with these statements:

1. When an artist composes a song, he or she owns it. It is their property. As a property owner, the artist has the right to control how it is used, reproduced, or distributed.
2. You can't reproduce or distribute music without the copyright owner's explicit permission.
3. You usually have to pay for their permission. Some artists may not charge, but you still have to get their permission.

Several decades ago, conscientious church musicians needed to individually contact songwriters and publishers for such permission. Imagine the frustration well-meaning people experienced on both ends.

Bob Kilpatrick, author of songs such as "(In My Life,) Lord, Be Glorified," describes the process:

> We would handle 25–50 requests each week from churches seeking permission to use "Lord, Be Glorified" in one way or another. We attempted to do this for free, but it became obvious that we were spending significant amounts of time, paper, and postage on it.

Churches found a great deal of inconsistency in the process and pricing when making such requests. Thankfully, times have changed.

Copyright Issues Now

Today, praise and worship leaders have an advocate: Christian Copyright Licensing International (CCLI). CCLI was founded in 1988 as a ministry and service to the church to educate the church about copyright laws, to protect the church from the consequences of copyright infringements, and to encourage greater utilization of copyrights in church services. CCLI contracts with hundreds of songwriters and publishers to handle the copyright issues on their behalf (and yours). In other words, CCLI makes it easy for you.

Just the Facts

Here's how it works: Your church purchases a renewable license, the price of which is based on a sliding scale according to the size of your church. The license allows you certain reproduction and usage rights on certain copyrighted Christian music. You periodically report to CCLI what songs you used and how you used them. CCLI then pays royalties to the copyright owners out of the license payments. You can learn more about how CCLI operates at their Website, *www.ccli.com.*

You don't *have* to obtain a license with CCLI to reproduce and use music in your church. You can always get permission the old-fashioned way, by writing to the songwriters and publishers. In the following section you will see common copyright questions based on real-world practices. The questions are each followed by two answers. One for those who don't obtain a CCLI license and one for those who do.

Straight Answers to the Most Frequently Asked Copyright Questions

Can I buy one copy of a collection or songbook, then photocopy and distribute the music to my musicians and/or singers?

1. **On your own:** No. Unless you obtain permission from the publisher, everyone who uses the music needs their own copy of the songbook. Imagine a choir of fifty people. Would it be okay if the choir director bought just one choral arrangement book, then made copies for everyone in the choir? Of course not. Everyone who uses the music to sing or perform needs their own copy.
2. **With a CCLI license:** No. The Church Copyright License does not convey the right to photocopy or duplicate any choral sheet music (octavos), cantatas, musicals, keyboard arrangements, vocal solos, or instrumental works. Everyone must own their own book.

We don't read music. Can I buy one collection or songbook, then make handwritten chord charts for my musicians and/or singers?

1. **On your own:** No. You are using the music, not just the book. Get permission.
2. **With a CCLI license:** Yes. CCLI will pay royalties to the publisher based on your reporting.

Can I make and reproduce my own chord charts or lead sheets if I play by ear or figure out the music by myself?

1. **On your own:** No. The songs still belong to the copyright holders. Each copyright holder may or may not allow you to do this. Get permission.
2. **With a CCLI license:** Yes. CCLI will pay royalties to the publisher based on your reporting.

On any given Sunday, my worship team and I might use music from three or four different songbooks. Shuffling bulky songbooks on and off our music stands is a bother. If I buy everyone on my worship team a copy of each songbook, can I then make photocopies of the music instead of using the songbooks?

1. **On your own:** Yes. Assuming you get permission from the publisher.
2. **With a CCLI license:** Yes.

Since the whole church is singing the song, do I have to buy a songbook for everyone in the congregation?

1. **On your own**: No.
2. **With a CCLI license:** No. A single song that is found in a collection of songs intended for congregational use (i.e., a hymnal or chorus book) can be copied into bulletins, congregational songbooks, congregational song sheets, or placed on a slide or transparency.

Can I make words-only overhead transparencies? Can we print the lyrics in a church bulletin?

1. **On your own:** Not without permission from the copyright holder.
2. **With a CCLI license:** Yes.

If I purchase a retail audiocassette or CD, can I make my own tapes, CDs, or MP3s of selected songs, then distribute them to my musicians and singers so they can learn the music prior to rehearsals?

1. **On your own**: No. You cannot duplicate and distribute retail recordings. Everyone needs their own purchased copy of the cassette or CD. No exceptions.
2. **With a CCLI license:** Same answer.

Wait a minute. We're using the music for worship. We're not selling or profiting financially from using it. Doesn't copyright law only apply in for-profit settings?

Sorry. This is a common misconception. The copyright owner is the only one who can decide whether or not to charge for reproduction and usage. You must obey the law whether you make money using the music or not.

Can our church group perform copyrighted music in a nonchurch setting (such as a coffeehouse) if we get paid? What if we don't charge?

1. **On your own:** Not without permission. Your compensation is irrelevant. The copyright holder has the right to control how and where their music is used.
2. **With a CCLI license:** CCLI does not cover music performance. If you are leading worship off the church grounds, and not charging fees, your CCLI license covers you. If, however, you *are* getting paid, that is a public performance and as such is not covered.

Do the Right Thing

Copyright laws exist to protect the artists. Everybody needs to make a living—even Christian recording artists. Consider what Lenny Smith, author of "Our God Reigns," said about CCLI:

CCLI has helped put three of my five children through college. The other two will also finish. When the churches send in their royalty payments, I hope they realize they are supporting songwriters who are real people with real bills much like their own!

The above information should settle in your mind what you can and cannot do with other people's music. If you have other questions about copyright law, we urge you to contact CCLI directly.

Now that we have spent some time considering issues associated with choosing music for your playlist and preparing the music for your team, let's return to the topic of arranging it so it results in a meaningful worship experience.

> Anyone, then, who knows the good he ought to do and doesn't do it, sins.
> JAMES 4:17

How to Arrange with Dynamics

By now, whenever you approach the task of generating a playlist, you are thinking about tempo family, content theme, and intended focus. Keeping these three items in mind will help you build excellent playlists. However, there's even more you can do. Let's begin with the importance of dynamics.

You're So Dynamic . . . or You Should Be

When I (Doug) was in high school, I went to many heavy-metal concerts. I remember the musicians would use enormous amplifiers and speaker systems. They would turn them all the way up, take the stage, and then start thrashing about at full volume for about ninety minutes. The music was loud, but it wasn't interesting, partly because it lacked dynamics.

Dynamics refers to the subtle and not-so-subtle changes in volume, speed, number of voices and/or instruments, and "attitude" that happen within a song. Dynamics help give a song a life of its own, a personality. As you arrange your music, plan for it to be dynamic. As my piano teacher used to tell me, "Put some feeling into it!"

Most hymns and modern choruses contain a verse and a chorus. At the most fundamental level, it is often a good idea to try to get your players and singers to perform the verse at about 85 percent volume, then play or sing the chorus at 100 percent. The subtle upsurge in volume will make your music more interesting.

Dynamics and Your Vocalists

As you glance over your playlist, envision how you might introduce variables into your vocal arrangements. Imagine a praise group with six singers: three men and three women.

While you could simply ask all six to sing all the time on all verses, think how much more dynamic it would be to mix it up. Consider this arrangement of "Holy, Holy, Holy."

Verse 1: Male soloist
Verse 2: Male/female duet, invite congregation to join in
Verse 3: Men and congregation on melody, all women sing harmony
Verse 4: Praise team sings four parts, congregation on melody

Introducing variables to your vocal parts adds enthusiasm and movement to your music.

How to Arrange with Mixed Instruments

It is boring to sing four verses in a row, all the same way. It is just as weak to arrange for all instruments to play all the time. When it is all instruments, all the time, all your songs end up sounding the same.

Think of an orchestra. Composers and conductors don't ask all the instruments to play all at once all the time, do they? Neither should you. Think of your worship team players as a mini orchestra. Try to come up with ways to add variables—even if you only have three instruments.

One effective strategy to use when arranging for your instruments has been called the "build as you go" method. Here's how it works: On the first verse, only one or two instruments play, and they play minimally. With each successive verse, you introduce additional instruments and patterns.

If you have ever heard the popular classical piece Pachelbel's Canon in D, you know exactly what we are talking about. Let's take the hymn "Holy, Holy, Holy" and study one way we could arrange the vocals and instruments with the "build as you go" method.

While you must let your creativity and ears be your guide, be careful to avoid this type of dramatic building on *every* song or your music will sound like a series

---

Arrangement Notes
"Holy, Holy, Holy"

Verse 1: Male soloist.
        Instrum: Keys only, thick chords, mostly half notes.

Verse 2: Male/Female duet, invite congregation to join in.
        Instrum: Add bass guitar, soft drums rim shot pattern.

Verse 3: Men & cong. on melody, all women sing harmony.
        Instrum: Add guitars, Drums change kick pattern.

Verse 4: Praise team sings 4 parts, cong. on melody.
        Instrum: Keys play more quarter notes, Drums add snare and ride cymbals.

of swells, sweeping up and down. It is much better to carefully and subtly craft it in. To give you a few ideas, here are a number of ways you can build with specific instruments:

Drums:
1. Simple kick with rim shot
2. Alternate kick with rim shot
3. Same kick, sub snare, add short rolls
4. Same kick, add longer rolls and crash cymbals

Guitar:
1. Finger pick
2. Soft strum with thumb
3. Strum softly with pick, add strokes
4. Full strum

Keys:
1. Hold most chords half to full measure
2. Move chords to different inversions between changes
3. Roll chords on quarter and/or eighth notes

Bass:
1. Stay on the root
2. Adding passing notes
3. Patterns in a higher register

To get an idea of how professionals do this, try to watch as many live performances as you can, even if they are only on TV. Study how the band works. Observe with your eyes and ears how different musicians dominate then back off. Listen to when the background singers blast and when they are quiet.

Hopefully, the ideas explained above will give you ideas on ways to dynamically build within a specific song. Now let's spend some time considering how to handle moving from one song to the next.

How to Arrange with Transitions and Segues to Get a Seamless Flow

As you arrange and subsequently lead music during worship, you will discover that there are two types of transitions you need to master. First, you will need to know how to smoothly get from one song to the next without interruption, maintaining the feel in the room. Secondly, you will need to know how to move from one song to the next while *changing* the feel in the room. We will refer to this latter type as "changing gears." Let's look at each in that order.

Getting from One Song to the Next without Interruption

You will want to do this whenever you have two or more songs with the same idea, feel, and style. For example:

"Holy Ground" to "We Are Standing on Holy Ground"
"He Is Exalted" to "Great Is the Lord"

In such instances you want to switch as smoothly as possible, where the first song flows directly, almost imperceptibly into the next. Smooth medleys are one of the distinguishing trademarks of contemporary praise and worship music. Think back to your earliest encounters with this form of worship. You were probably delighted with the way the leaders drifted from song to song in a series of mini-medleys. Sometimes, the two songs are conveniently in the same key. At other times, you will need to modulate. Let's look at both instances.

Seamless Transitions without a Key Change

These are easy. When you are arranging two songs back to back where both are in the same key, you give the congregation a warning, then simply play right into the second song. It is important to let the congregation know that a new song is coming, even if your visual aids clearly indicate there is about to be a change.

Always warn people right before you switch to a different song.

Many worship leaders miss this important leadership step. When you instantly switch to a new song without warning your congregation, some of your people will inevitably be surprised or embarrassed, especially anyone singing with their eyes closed! Here's the secret to providing a smooth transition: You talk on top of the music during the last measure of the first song. That's right. While everyone else is singing the last measure of the first song, you talk—giving instructions. Consider this example of two popular songs that work well together. The vertical lines indicate the measures.

End of "He Is Exalted"

All: . . . on high. | He is exalted, the | King is exalted on | high!

You: . . . on high. | He is exalted, the | King is exalted on | "Let's sing 'Great Is the Lord'"

(You sing this part)   (You speak here)

All: Great is the Lord, He is | holy and just . . .

You: Great is the Lord, He is | holy and just . . .

(You sing this part)

Since "He Is Exalted" and "Great Is the Lord" are both in the same time signature (6/8) and roughly the same tempo, there is no need to play an introduction for the latter. You simply provide the verbal warning or cue, then play right into it.

Transitions with a Key Change

There will be other times in your arrangements where you will have two songs back to back, but you will need to change keys to get from one to the other. In the first chapter we learned how to modulate, or change keys, between songs, so there is no need to repeat the instructions here. If modulating is new to you, study that chapter until you are comfortable adding modulation measures and moving smoothly between keys.

When you need to change keys, you simply add your modulation measures, then, depending on how much you have to say, talk on top of them, instead of or in addition to the final measure of the first song. The modulation measures also give your congregation an "audio warning" that something is about to change.

Here is a chord chart example of a transition that requires a modulation. In this example, you move from "We Bring the Sacrifice of Praise" (in D) to "Come into His Presence with Thanksgiving in Your Heart" (in B♭). Notice when the leader stops singing and starts talking.

(Song ending)   *(Modulation meas)* *(New song)*

Bm7   F#m7 G/A A D   Cm Cm E♭/F E♭/F   B♭   BbMaj7

All: The sacri | fices of | joy. | . . . . | Come into His presence.

You: "Let's come into his presence!"

(Spoken here)

That covers moving from one song to the next when both are in the same key and both are in the same tempo family. We have also covered how to move from one song to the next when both are in the same tempo family, but in two different keys.

Now let's examine techniques you can use when you want to move from one song to the next while changing the feel in the room.

Changing Gears in Your Worship Service

Picture a wonderful, peaceful worship segment where your congregation seems gently cradled in the arms of Jesus. There's a comforting sense of hush as eyes are closed and voices are quietly lifted. As wonderful as this experience is, you also want the worship service to contain an element of rock-solid confidence, where the church corporately affirms the truth of the gospel.

How in the world are you going to break one mood and move into the next? After all, there are times when you want to create an "atmospheric shift" in the service. For example, you just finished a time of exuberant, hand-clapping enthusiasm, and you need to quiet the people down because a season of focused prayer is coming in the service. This is a little tricky because you need to steer people, but you want to do it without their noticing.

Many worship leaders fail here. What does it feel like to your passengers when you are driving a car and suddenly slam on the brakes? That's what it is like for worshipers when there are abrupt changes in the atmosphere during worship. While you will of course need to change direction in a service, your goal is to segue smoothly.

While there are many ways to do this, perhaps the worst is to simply slam into the next set or medley. Rapid-fire changes from one tempo family to the next rarely work well. What you need is a bridge.

Between the Tempo Families

The "space" between two tempo families in your playlist is something you need to manage carefully. What you will find in the next few paragraphs are techniques professional worship leaders have found useful.

Talk Your Way across the Tempo Families

This is by far the most common method. As soon as a song stops, start talking. Use your voice, dynamics, and pitch just like a preacher does. Start with your voice in the same "attitude" as the last song. Need to slow down? Gradually lower your volume and speed throughout your paragraph. Need to wind it up? Increase the excitement and pitch in your voice with each sentence. During your talking transition, be sure your band is watching for your cue to start the next song.

Stand or Sit

The physical movement of your congregation getting up "because it's gonna get rowdy in here!" or sitting down to cool off and relax is a great way to segue.

Clap

We think clapping works best after finishing a faster set of songs because it's natural to want to applaud after an enthusiastic experience! The predictable, gradual dying off of the applause is a perfect way to downshift into a more moderate tempo family. On occasion, we have seen clapping work after a slow set or at the start of a service too. Once during a particularly somber and focused period of worship, the leader quickly shifted into a higher gear by steadily increasing the speed and pitch of his voice as he concluded a quiet prayer and immediately addressed the people with something along these lines:

"Let's lift up the Lord with a praise offering!"
    (Starts clapping his hands, musicians quickly join in)
"Yes! Lift up the Lord!"
    (Clapping and voice intensifies)
"It's time to shout to the Lord with a voice of triumph!"
    (Cues bass guitar—eighth notes at 120 bpm, congregation starts clapping in rhythm with bass—drums start. . .)

You get the idea. In about forty seconds, the congregation has moved swiftly and successfully to a different tempo family. Boy, that guy was smooth.

Musical Interlude That Changes

Another terrific method is to let the instruments create the bridge. As always, warn the congregation to "just listen to the instruments as we continue in worship." As they do, the band either cranks it up or cools it off, which is very effective. Once the new tempo is achieved, the worship leader again addresses the people.

If you are the type of player who can play and talk at the same time, you are seriously blessed. It is practical to improvise, or vamp, between songs and tempo families, steadily changing the feel while talking or reading a brief Scripture passage.

Key Change

If you need only make a minor adjustment to tempo, try using a series of modulation measures—at least two—and adjust tempo during the modulation.

QUICK TIPS: DO'S AND DON'TS FOR ARRANGING WORSHIP MUSIC

In this final section of this chapter you will find a series of ideas, tips, tricks, and tools of the trade used by professional music arrangers. Read them all, then pick and choose the strategies that make sense in your unique setting.

Don't Repeat a Song Unless You Also Provide a Musical Reason to Do So

We once heard a workshop leader give this sage advice: When you play and sing a song through, don't repeat it in the same way just for the sake of doing it again. Instead of playing the same song over and over with the same musical arrangement, use the "build as you go" strategy with either the instruments and/or the vocal arrangements. On each successive repeat, add an instrument, change the vocal arrangement, vary the drum pattern, or play it an octave higher.

Never Teach a Song with a Tricky Melody As the First Song in the Service

You are probably reading this right now partly because you just love praise and worship music. Your CD collection is likely rather vast. You regularly hear songs that really minister to you personally, and consequently, you want to teach them to your church. Way to go. But think before you teach.

It is risky to open your worship service by teaching a new song, but it is not impossible. Actually, if you have good rapport with your people, this can be effective. Just make sure the "cool new song" you're teaching is easy to sing. Here's a rule of thumb: If the melody moves around a lot, use it as a performance piece first. If you can't tell, test the new song on your worship team at the beginning of a rehearsal. If they struggle with it, your congregation will have an even harder time.

Don't Stay in the Same Key for More Than Three Songs

Everybody has their own pet key. I (Doug) love to sing and play in A♭ and D♭. Whenever I sing a solo, I try to sing it in either A♭ or D♭. However, if I led my congregation in a playlist where all the songs were in A♭, things would get pretty boring. Try to move into different keys throughout your playlist. If you don't, your music will become uninteresting. By the way, guitarists—help your keyboardists. Learn to play the flat keys too!

Let Others on the Team Read Scripture, Introduce Songs, Etc.

Don't be a one-man show. While we are sure you are blessed with talent, a nice voice, and good communication skills, you should let others on your team take roles in the elements of the worship service. Is there a good reason that an alto can't read the Scripture? Why can't the drummer introduce a song? Let the bassist lead in prayer once in a while. Part of being a leader is being an equipper.

Don't Make Your People Feel Like Popcorn.

Stand up. Sing. Sit down. Listen. Stand up. Clap. Sit down. Sing. Stand up. Pray. Sit down.

Get the idea? Cut it out.

Survey Says . . .

Every once in a while, print a list of the praise and worship songs you use at your church. Put this list in the bulletin and ask the congregation to place a check mark next to their favorites, then use them. This can be a real eye-opener.

Don't Stop after Every Song

Contemporary praise and worship music tends to be characterized by short songs and choruses. We have been in churches where the music leader will sing a quick two-minute chorus, then come to a full stop, say a few words, then rev up another two-minute chorus, then stop. Don't do this. Worship choruses and songs are more like slides than painted murals. They work best when they follow one another rather quickly. One of the best things you can do is learn to create medleys of praise and worship songs and choruses.

Keep Your Planning Sheets

As you seek to locate songs with specific themes and tempos, and create planning lists of song candidates, don't throw away your notes! If you work on paper, just place your planning notes into a file folder and keep them. Six months from now, you'll be glad you did. If you work on a computer and create a personal database, don't forget to create backups.

Don't Ask People to Clap Too Much

Asking people to clap for more than about four minutes is asking for trouble. Even though they might be into it, hands tend to tire. If people want to spontaneously clap along, by all means let them, but don't make them feel as if they *must* clap for more than one or two choruses.

If You Want Them to Clap . . .

One more thing about clapping. Have you ever been in a congregation when someone tried to get clapping going, but it just didn't work? Ever wonder why? If you want people to clap, make sure the tempo of the song you are doing is between 100 and 130 bpm. If the song is slower, they won't clap. If it is much faster, they will get tired and quit on you.

You Don't Need to Have the Congregation Sing Every Song in Your Set

While many churches like to punctuate singing with testimonies and other service events, we find worship services most meaningful when there's a block of time dedicated just to music, prayer, and Scripture readings.

If you are blessed to enjoy serving in a church where the leadership encourages twenty to forty minutes of worship ministry, remember that you don't have to ask the congregation to sing every song.

Here's why: People get tired. Have the congregation sing two to three choruses in a medley. Then, give the congregation a break and let just the worship team take a song, or perhaps give a piece to a soloist. You might want to divide a song where your worship team sings the more difficult verse, then ask the congregation to join in on the chorus. Think about the way the original artists perform "God Is the Strength of My Heart" and "God Will Make a Way." In each case, the leader sings the verse and the congregation sings the chorus.

Limit Slow Songs

Be careful using slow songs. It's probable you won't want to use more than two or three slow songs after another in a medley. Be especially careful if the slow songs are in minor keys. If you have several slow songs you want to do together, break them up in your set with a verbal transition where you might explain why a song was written or why you chose it, or where you offer a deep, yet relevant, theological comment. Odds are, if you try to sing three slow songs in a row, children will get fidgety and the adults in the congregation will get tired.

Start Sunday Morning in a Lower Key

Many people have trouble singing high notes early in the morning. Don't worry about why. It just is. So, if you can, avoid songs that take people above the B♭ above middle C early on Sunday morning. Why? If people try to hit a high note and their voice cracks, they suddenly become horribly self-conscious, and for them, worship is over. However, if you keep the first song or two low, people will sing more confidently and enthusiastically. We guarantee it.

Avoid Time-Signature Changes within a Given Set of Songs

Once people start singing in 4/4, they tend to want to keep singing in 4/4. Also, if you have less experienced musicians on your team, switching time signatures can cause panic attacks. There's nothing wrong with using different time signatures during a service, we have simply found it better for everyone if you schedule a break between changing time signatures. Here are two examples.

First the less desirable way:

Song 1: (3/4) "Turn Your Eyes upon Jesus"
Song 2: (4/4) "Think about His Love"
Song 3: (6/8) "Jesus, Name above All Names"

With this arrangement, you have three great songs, but the time signature keeps changing. No matter how smooth your transitions, some people are likely to get frustrated, and not even know why! Here's a better way to move through three different time signatures:

Song 1: (3/4) "We Will Glorify"
Song 2: (3/4) "Turn Your Eyes upon Jesus"

Stop singing, play a transition as you talk briefly about God's love. Then lead into the next songs. . .

Song 3: (4/4) "Think about His Love"
Song 4: (4/4) "In His Presence"

Stop singing. Play transition as you read a Scripture passage about lifting up the Lord.

Song 5: (6/8) "Jesus, Name above All Names"
Song 6: (6/8) "He Is Exalted"

Avoid Overdoing Novelty Songs

Let's face it. Some of the praise and worship music you hear on popular recordings is just plain gimmicky. There is nothing wrong with this type of music as long as it isn't overdone. Of course, it is true that the definition of "novelty" varies widely by region. But consider for example the worship leader in a predominantly white suburban church. For her, there are only so many marches, reggae, Yiddish, Latino, and foreign language songs her congregation can handle.

On a related note, don't make the mistake of superimposing your own musical tastes on your congregation. You say you love Celtic music? Fine. Don't bring too much of it to church. Ska ministers to you? Okay, but realize some people can't stand that stuff.

Use the Internet to Locate the Right Song

Don't forget to use the Internet. If you have a specific worship theme, use your Web search engine to find new stuff. You never know what might turn up. There are many, many resources such as indexes, databases, and hymn and chorus concordances available online. Get used to using them. For example, you might want to try key words like "worship song database," "worship music," etc.

What Kind of Atmosphere Do You Want When Worship Singing Ends?

A good way to wind up your playlist is to ask yourself this question: *What in the service follows the singing?*

If it's the "stand up and greet each other" segment or announcements, you probably want to end your music package on a note of exuberance, not reflection. On the other hand, if the pastoral prayer or communion comes next, you will want a more contemplative, not excited, atmosphere.

Bear with us for this metaphor. The congregation is almost like a football you hand off to the leader of the next element in the service. If the next service element is a more quiet, serious one, you don't want to pass the congregation off with their hearts racing because they just sang a wild, fast song. Think about what comes next when compiling playlists.

Keep Good Records of the Music You Use

Finally, make sure you keep track of what music you use. Not only will you need to compile this data periodically if you use CCLI, but you will also find it interesting to track how often you do a specific song. One idea is to simply jot the date on the back of your music before you file it away.

in CLoSing

Congratulations! You have covered plenty of ground in this chapter. Before you move on, there is one final assignment: Keeping your finger in this spot, glance back through this chapter and write yourself a reminder of several things you most want to apply. Do it right now, so you don't forget.

Things I Need to Apply from This Chapter:

1. _____ (page _____)

2. _____ (page _____)

3. _____ (page _____)

4. _____ (page _____)

5. _____ (page _____)

chapter 3

give Your singers a Tune-up

in This chapter You Will Learn

- How to help your singers develop a clean sound.
- The top ten clear communication tips.
- How to teach your singers to stay in shape.
- Helps for singers on the platform.
- Quick tips: do's and don'ts for singers.

introduction to This chapter

In 1 Corinthians, the apostle Paul makes a comment on church music.

> I will sing with my spirit, but I will also sing with my mind. If you are praising God with your spirit, how can one who finds himself among those who do not understand say "Amen" to your thanksgiving, since he does not know what you are saying?
>
> 1 CORINTHIANS 14:15–16

This is an important passage for those of us who use music in the church because it is about singing. We will let the biblical scholars debate the precise meaning of this passage and the proper application of spiritual gifts. For the purpose of this chapter, the spiritual gifts issue is a sidebar. Wherever you might be on the theological continuum, we think it is safe to say that at a minimum, a major emphasis of this section of Scripture could be summed up with these three points:

1. When it comes to communicating or ministering with song, singers need to be understood.
2. Being understood enables people to engage in the worship experience.
3. If people don't understand us, what's the point?

Your singers already have good voices; that's why they sing. This chapter is designed to help you do all you can to informally, casually, and subtly fine-tune them. Whether you want your singers to sound formally trained like Sandi Patti and Celine Dion, or earthy and gutsy like Rebecca St. James and Sheryl Crow, they need to sing correctly.

how to help your Singers Develop a clean Sound

Do you know the song "Louie, Louie" by the Kingsmen? Sing along in your head as you read the lyrics below.

> *Louie, Louie, oh, baby. We gotta go now.*
> *Yeah, yeah, yeah, yeah, yeah, yeah.*
> *Louie, Louie, oh, baby. We gotta go now.*
> *Yeah, yeah, yeah, yeah, yeah, yeah.*

Now. What comes next? I'll bet you don't know.
No one does.

As great a groove as that song might have, the rest of the lyrics are unintelligible to most people. That might be okay in pop songs, but when it comes to leading in worship, it just won't do. The apostle Paul, writing under the influence of the Holy Spirit, instructs us that we need to sing so people will understand what we are saying.

As a worship leader, it is likely that you will sing at least part of the time. You will also have the awesome responsibility of directing people who sing. It is part of your job to make sure that the people in the congregation can understand what's being sung.

Let's get this straight before we begin: There is no substitute for professional voice training. Now let's face reality: Some of your singers are never going to take lessons. Hopefully, you will be able to take some of the ideas presented in this chapter, some of it contributed by professional vocal instructor Audrey Hunt of The Audrey Hunt Vocal Company, and deliver it to your singers.

While this chapter can't substitute for formal instruction with a qualified teacher, it does cover a number of key areas that can make a big difference in the quality of your sound.

Singing Style

We don't know about you, but we get frustrated when a singer's "style" is such that we can't understand the lyrics. While we don't want to diminish anyone's artistic style, we know that some artists are better than others when it comes to communicating. It is our contention that anyone leading worship should strive for clarity, so they can be understood.

It is also our impression that some casual and/or contemporary singers hide their lack of skill and technique behind their "style." Sloppy singing should never be tolerated. Make this the bottom line for yourself and your singers: If you're going to sing in church, you had better be understood. Being understood begins with good pronunciation, enunciation, and diction.

Ouch! That Hurt

As you work with your singers, it is highly likely you will notice they sometimes exhibit bad habits in their singing. It is not your role to become headmaster of the vocal sin squad, pointing out every foible your singers unknowingly exhibit. However, you will want to develop an atmosphere at your rehearsals where correction regularly (and gently) takes place.

Take 5

As a worship leader, you might open your rehearsals with five (and only five) minutes of instruction, where you teach one of the principles in this chapter per week. If you do, over the course of a year, each one will get covered five times. Not only will you look smart when you start throwing around terms like *labial consonants,* but you will hear a payoff in your group's sound.

The Top Ten cLeaR communication TIps

I (Tami) love to hear people speak French. It is such a lovely spoken language. For singing, Italian is probably the most beautiful. Where does English rank in the world of singing? Somewhere in the middle. Consequently, the sounds of the English language need to be carefully controlled when sung because some of the sounds are beautiful and others are downright ugly. One of the keys to singing for understanding is learning what to do with each type of sound. Here are some tips you should learn. Follow them yourself, then teach them to your singers. By the way, we are well aware we could be much more technical and phonetically detailed, but if we did, you probably wouldn't read on. This is the important stuff you need to get your singers doing.

In the sections that follow, you will find the ten most important techniques you can get your singers to practice. If you can get all of your singers to follow these principles, you and your congregation will notice a dramatic increase in sound quality.

Tip #1: Eliminate the Vibrato

The vibrato is the wiggle in your voice that you and your singers probably add spontaneously on anything longer than quarter notes. When singing alone, the vibrato can be a wonderfully expressive tool. When singing in a group, it can lead to a mushy sound.

The problem is twofold. First, when two or more people are singing with vibrato, they often wiggle at different speeds. When this happens, you diminish the clarity of the sound. Second, people use vibrato with different degrees of intensity. Some people vary the pitch in their voice just a little, while others vary pitch much wider. Again, two people with different degrees of depth—what do you think you get? You guessed it: mush.

Instruct your singers to do all they can to produce a smooth, solid, clean tone—without vibrato. They should endeavor to sing as smoothly as possible when singing in a group. Remind them that when they are singing a solo, they can feel free to vibrato off into the sunset. However, when blending with a group, a solid, clean tone is the goal.

One good way to emphasize this is to demo it. Instead of you singing "the right way," let someone else do it. Bring to your rehearsals CDs by acappella groups like Take6, Acappella, Manhatten Transfer, and Glad. Play a few cuts and tell your singers to listen to the blended voices. Do they hear vibrato? Nope. Sure, sometimes the voice in the forefront (on melody) adds some in for interest, but the blended voices are almost always solid, clean bell-like tones. That's what you want too.

Tip #2: Read the Lyrics Out Loud First

Before they come to rehearsal, get your singers to privately read aloud the lyrics they will be singing. As they do, encourage them to do so as if they were dramatic readers. They should ask themselves to figure out how to read the lyrics expressively. This will enable them to do a number of things.

First, it will personalize the music for them. As they read they will begin to understand where and how the songwriter felt the emotion, which will benefit their singing. Second, they will begin to see where they should breathe. Tell your singers to note where they breathe when reading the lyrics because that's where they should breathe when singing. They might even use a pencil to place check marks where they are to breathe. Finally, it will help your singers perfect their pronunciation. They might even taperecord their dramatic readings, then listen to themselves. This can be a real eye- (or ear-) opener.

Tip #3: When Holding a Note, Hold the Vowel

As mentioned before, it is sad but true: When sung, English simply is not among the most beautiful of languages. Consequently, we must do things to emphasize the better sounds. Fortunately, English vowels do sound rather nice. Since they sound nice, emphasize them.

There is another reason why you want your singers to emphasize the vowels. Singing a vowel requires your mouth to be open resulting in a smoother sound. On the other hand, singing or speaking consonants requires the mouth to be partially closed or blocked. When your mouth is open, the quality of sound is typically better than when it is closed or even partially closed.

Tip #4: Overenunciate Dental Consonants

In the English language there are different types of consonants. Professional singers have identified specific techniques for singing each type that maximizes tonal quality. *Dental consonants* are the ones that require the use of the teeth to form. *D, T,* and *Th* are three examples. How do you handle dental consonants when singing? You *over*enunciate them, but bring them to a rapid close. This is especially important when they come at the end of a lyric.

When your singers fail to sing dental consonants cleanly, a mushy sound results. This is compounded when a group of singers is involved. Think about times you have heard a song on the radio where you couldn't sing along because you couldn't understand the lyrics. Chances are, part of the problem was poor enunciation. Dental consonants are frequently sung poorly.

When dental consonants are not consciously and deliberately included as part of the lyric, they can sound like this:

"That" becomes "Thaaa"
"Would" becomes "Wuuuuh"
"Happened" becomes "Happeeeen"
"Battle" becomes "Baddul"

All of the above and countless others become sloppy. Unintelligible. Unacceptable. Make sure your singers literally feel their tongue touch their teeth. That's the nature of enunciation! One more thing, if you are working with a group of singers, rehearse clipping the dental consonants at exactly the same place. Make sure everyone does it together. You don't want a *t-t-t* sound.

> When a GROuP Is SINGING, ReHeaRSe CLIPPING the Dental ConsonanTS at the Same PLaCe.

At a rehearsal, ask your singers to first speak, then sing the following words. Encourage them to deliberately observe the way their tongue touches their teeth. Then instruct them to overenunciate words like these when singing:

Don't
Didn't
Tried
Mighty is our God

Your goal is to get them to sound crisp. Right now, try singing these examples of phrases from well-known hymns to reinforce what we are talking about. Practice feeling your tongue touching the teeth.

"Take time to be holy . . ."
"Day by day and with each passing moment . . ."

Tip #5: Underenunciate Nasal Consonants

You guessed it; *nasal consonants* need the nose. *M* and *N* are the two nasal consonants. Try pronouncing both right now. Where did the sound come from? It came from your nose, didn't it?

The problem immediately becomes apparent when you remember that singing through your nose is a bad idea. Few tones from the human body sound more vulgar than singing through the nose.

So what's a singer to do with nasal consonants? *Under*enunciate them. In other words, tell your singers to sing them a little softer. You might suggest singing them at 75 percent volume. Form them quickly, then just as quickly get to the vowel. As in the previous section, let's reinforce this right now.

First try speaking, then singing the following words and phrases two ways. First, incorrectly as you *stay* on the nasal consonant. Listen to how ugly that sounds! Then speak and sing them a second time, quickly exiting off the nasal consonant. What a difference!

> Some vocal teachers like to instruct singers to sing words starting with P, B, F, and V as if they were lower-case, just slightly softer than normal.

Moment
Minute
Number
Mary, did you know?
Make me new . . .

Tip #6: Hold Back When Singing Labial Consonants

Labial means "lip." *Labial consonants* are the letters you need your lips to make. There are two pure labial consonants, *P* and *B*, and two labial dentals, *F* and *V*, which require both tongue and lips.

Hold back just a little when singing these. If you don't, they can sound explosive, especially if you sing close to the microphones. If you hold back just a little, and use less air, you can eliminate that irritating pop that echoes through the speaker system when labial consonants are incorrectly sung.

You try it. As before, speak, then sing the following words and phrases. First use a hard labial (lots of air); then do it again, this time with less air. Feel the difference? When singing with a group, always encourage people to hold back just a little and watch what happens to the blend!

Victory
Parable
Believe
Faithful
Praise the name of Jesus
Blessed be the powerful One

Tip #7: Never, Never Hang On to Pneumatic Consonants!

We know we are using slang here, but it makes the point. We like to call these sounds "hissers." Actually the formal name is *pneumatics* because they require a gush of air to make the sound.

Try saying these right now and you'll see what we mean: *S, Sh, Z, Th, Ch, cks, ks, K, J.*

Never stay or hang on hissers or pneumatic consonants. If you do, you'll get the following repellent sounds:

Hold on to *S*, and you'll sound like air going out of a tire.
Hold on to *Sh*, and you'll end up hushing the baby.
Hold on to *Z*, and you'll attract bumblebees.
Hold on to *Th*, and you'll thound aths if you thing with a lithsp.
Hold on to *Ch*, and you'll sound like you left the water running.

Here's a few examples to use in your training with your singers:

Attacks
Sustaineth
Church's
Thanks

Try singing (and holding) the word *because* two ways:
First, emphasize or hold the *Z* sound. Hear how bad that sounds?
Second, emphasize the *au* and squeak the *Z* in at the last nanosecond. That's better.

Tip #8: What About "R"?

How do you sing the letter *R?* Honestly, it is one of the hardest letters to sing.

Vocal teachers debate the best way to sing it. Some recommend rolling the letter *R* every time it's encountered. Well, most people who listen to adult contemporary music won't appreciate this (unless you're singing in Spanish or within Latino-oriented cultures). Others say you only pronounce the *R* sound if it appears at the beginning or in the middle of the word. When the word ends in an *R*, it is best to ignore it, and sing as if it's not there.

Try singing this word: *Remember.*

Did you hold on to the *rrrrrrr* sound at the end? Most listeners find the *R* sound at the end of a word unpleasant. We agree.

Instead, try singing the word with the pronunciation "remembuh." Don't over emphasize the ending of words like these. Purse your lips a little and get softer at the end; it will sound much nicer! Here are a few more words to try. Sing them with a hard *R* on the end. Then sing them again substituting the *uh* sound. Which sounds better to you?

Over
Closer
Believer
Nearer
Sure

Whichever method you decide, hard *R* or softened *uh,* make sure all your singers do the same thing.

Tip #9: Double-Check the Pronunciation of Words

Depending on where you live, you might pronounce words differently when singing and speaking. For example, make up a melody and sing this phrase: "Of this I am sure. . ."

Does *sure* rhyme with *her* or *poor?* Try it both ways. It makes a difference doesn't it?

Sing "I know this because . . ." Does the second syllable of *because* sound like *buzz* or *saws?*

Here's another one that just might split your church: Does *amen* sound like *aye-men* or *ah-men?*

Now we could spend several pages trying to persuade you to pronounce it correctly (the way we do on the East Coast), but we'll skip it. The important thing to remember is that when singing in a small group, everyone must pronounce it the same way.

Tip #10: Communicate Emotionally

Get your singers to aim at telling the story of each song to the audience, making your lyrics both eloquent and easily understood.

This is especially important if your group is singing a song that is well-known in your church. It's easy to slip into autopilot and just sing through it without thinking about the message. Remind your singers that they are making statements to God and the people in the congregation. They should view their ministry as an art form—an exercise in skillful, deep communication.

Sure, some people overwork a song and end up looking plastic, artificial, and just plain silly. Others are so stiff and void of emotion observers wonder if they are cardboard cutouts. Obviously we want to avoid both extremes and think about what we are communicating and display the appropriate amount of emotion. Remind your singers to do less performing and more worshiping.

One good way to communicate this to your singers is to videotape them in action. Your camcorder can be your best adjunct professor. You can talk about platform presence and presentation all day long, but when your singers actually see themselves on stage wearing a deadpan expression, it'll change them.

How to Teach Your Singers to Stay in Shape

Your singers need to know that their number one responsibility is keeping their voice in top condition. Help them understand that an important component of this is staying in good physical condition.

Explain that just as a guitar needs to be regularly tuned to maintain its sound, the voice needs regular and systematic "tuning" to stay in good form. Some guitars don't need to be tuned every day, but few can go for more than two or three without a refresh. The singer's physical body is the same way.

Imagine what would happen to a dancer, for example, if that dancer were to take a break and stop working out for any given period of time. Yet there are some singers who have not learned the value of regular exercise.

Let's Get Physical

Physical exercise will improve any singer's voice by improving cardiovascular strength, breath stamina, and strengthening overall muscle tone. Exercise also stimulates your endorphins.

Also, if a singer's muscles are out of shape, it is more difficult to support their breath or sing with rich, powerful tones. Vocal cords are an extension of the body; therefore, singers must constantly work on good muscle tone. If you are out of shape, injured, or tense, you actually restrict your ability to sing to your full potential.

Audrey Hunt observes,

> It has been my experience that whenever a singer, amateur or professional, complains of a tight gripping feeling in the throat, hoarseness, a sore throat, lack of range, or shortness of breath, the problem is poor physical condition or mental stress.

Encourage your singers to do some form of aerobic activity every day to develop a great set of lungs and prepare the body for the stamina that a singer must have. And don't forget to lead by example!

Encouraging Private Practice Sessions

For singers, physical and vocal exercise are important. If you want your singers to sound their best, it is imperative that you do everything you can to get your singers to sing every day. While it is probably unrealistic to expect them to engage in a professional vocal workout every day, they should sing at least a little on a daily basis.

Your singers need to understand that their voice is their instrument. Just like the players in your praise and worship band need to practice during the week, your singers need to do more than simply show up for one midweek rehearsal and Sunday services.

The beautiful thing about being a singer is that you can use your instrument anywhere, at any time. Encourage your singers to sing at least fifteen minutes a day. It doesn't matter when or where they practice—in the shower, while driving, or puttering around the house. When they sing though, encourage them to make the most of the opportunity.

A casual daily practice session can be compared to an exercise routine where you warm up before you work out. Applying the following guidelines can help a marginal singer experience rapid progress, and a good singer sound great.

Warm-Up: When you are ready to start, begin by humming a scale or simple tune lightly and quietly. This wakes up the vocal cords and lets them know a workout is coming. This should take two to three minutes, but don't rush this part.

Workout: It is a good idea to start your workout phase by singing scales. Some professional voice teachers get carried away with scales, forcing their students to sing them hour after hour. Unless you are working with a professional teacher, singing scales endlessly can actually do more harm than good, due to the fatigue. You derive plenty of benefit if you simply sing a few scales, softly yet deliberately, then move on to a song.

Next, choose a song or hymn that's popular at your church and start singing it. Start in a key that's easy on your voice. One or two verses should suffice. Not too loudly though. Once you feel warmed up and ready, it's time to branch out gently from your natural, easy vocal register.

Most people instinctively know where their comfort range is. The goal of your daily vocal workout is to gently but deliberately stretch your voice, but not too much.

Some people think a loud voice is the same thing as a powerful voice. Nothing is further from the truth. Loud is just loud. Pushing your voice too hard will only strain it. Also when trying to sing loud, the airflow is forced too hard, which almost always pulls the notes sharp. This probably isn't a problem with gentle songs like "As the Deer" and "Joy of My Desire"; however, when some singers get to exuberant pieces like "Celebrate Jesus" or the "Victory Chant," they end up belting it out Ethel Merman style. It is much better to hold back a little and let the microphone do some of the hard work.

PUSHING YOUR VOICE too HARD WILL ONLY STRAIN IT.

During your daily vocal workout try to gently move up and down the scale, just outside your comfort range. One suggestion is to sing your favorite song, but move the key up on successive verses. In other words, sing your workout song in the key of C the first time, then move up to D. When you feel you are moving into difficult territory, don't push it. Your range and tone will improve with gradual, gentle stretching.

hELPS FOR SINGERS ON the PLAtfORM

In addition to working with your singers during rehearsals and encouraging them to work on their own during the week, there are a number of things you can do to help them when it is time to minister.

What Beverage Is Best to Soothe a Scratchy Throat?

It is probably a good idea for your singers to subtly hide a small beverage to sip on if they get a tickle in their throat while on the platform.

Naturally, the important question is, What should be in the cup?

- Ice water?
- Syrupy fruit juice?
- Carbonated soda?
- Milk?
- Hot coffee?
- Warm tea?

In other words, what works *best* at quickly quieting an irritated set of vocal cords? The verdict is in: room temperature water.

While many singers might swear by other remedies, most professionals would agree that room temperature water is best. There are several problems with other beverages. Ice water causes vocal cords to shrink, constrict, and even numb, making it harder to control your voice. Why do you put ice on a bruise? To shrink it down. This is the exact opposite of what you want to do to your vocal cords.

What about syrupy beverages such as fruit juices? Sugary drinks like fruit juice and punch should be avoided because the molecular particles of syrup tend to coat the back of the throat, restricting control. What about tart drinks like lemonade and lemon water? Although often mistakenly endorsed, the citric acid in tart drinks can create a tightening effect on the muscles in your mouth and throat. Carbonated soda or pop? Do we really need to talk about gas in your stomach while singing? Stay away! By all means stay away from milk and cheese before you sing. They form mucous in your throat. Needless to say, you don't want a throat full of mucous while you sing.

Finally, how about a nice cup of coffee during singing? Coffee while singing is the worst of all. First, if it is hot, you will irritate your tongue and throat, and make both swell or expand slightly. You only compound the trouble if you add cream and sugar. Now it is probably okay for your singers to start their Sunday morning with a cup of coffee, assuming they won't be singing right after they jump out of bed. What we are talking about here is drinking coffee in the warm-up room *right before* they sing. That is a no-no.

Let's be clear here: Drink room temperature water before and while singing. Save other beverages until after you are finished singing.

Choosing a Good Microphone

When it comes to microphones, like many things in life, you get what you pay for. Every microphone has its own personality, which picks up different frequencies and textures in the user's voice. The right mic can make your voice soar. The wrong one can make you sound like a cartoon character. Once you find one that works best for you, stick with it.

A microphone will not enhance your sound; it will only project what you already have. For example, if you mispronounce a vowel, everyone will hear it, or it will show up on the recording. If your voice is breathy, that too will be heard. So it is in your best interest to get the very best microphones you can afford and be technically prepared to use them well.

Microphones can be divided into two broad categories. On the one hand there are those best used for recording; on the other, microphones for performing. Vocal coach Audrey Hunt offers the following field guide to becoming acquainted with popular microphones.

Microphones for Performing

Shure SM57, SM58: These industry standard microphones were designed for live performance. They offer a warm tone, excellent durability, and predictability.

Shure EL76: Another popular microphone for stage use.

AKG 414, 412: These are good, popular microphones that tend to accentuate frequencies on the high end, resulting in a brighter sound. Consequently, professional engineers and sound technicians often use them for voices that require additional sparkle. Considered ideal for warm, dark alto and bass voices. Not so good, however, for a high clean voice since many feel they lack the warmth of tone needed for such a voice.

Microphones for Recording

Sennheiser 421: A reasonable basic recording microphone, often found in low-budget recording studios, this is not the best choice for the serious singer. Originally designed for broadcasting.

Top-of-the-Line Microphones

There are three types of microphone designs: condenser, ribbon, and dynamic. The better mics described below are those with condenser and/or ribbon. The condenser mics come in two versions, a field-effect-transistor (FET) and a tube, which is the highest quality you can have for recording. Among the most popular professional studio mics you will encounter are those manufactured by Neumann.

Neumann U87: A great all-around FET condenser mic. Good depth and color to the tone, with great highs and mid-range. Very well balanced.

Neumann U67: The tube version of U87. One step up in quality (and price).

Neumann 47 series: A warmer version mic than the 87, giving a fuller bottom sound on the voice. It is available in both FET and tube designs.

Good Microphone Technique

When you and your singers use your microphones, keep these helpful tips in mind:

1. Avoid touching the grill of the microphone. Hand oil, dirt, and products such as lipstick can leak into the grill. Using a foam windscreen will help.
2. Hold the microphone at such an angle that you sing directly into the top of the microphone head. Your voice will always sound better this way.
3. Do not "eat" the microphone. This will distort the sound. It doesn't matter how your favorite singer leans into and onto their microphone in the video. Keep your lips to yourself.
4. Avoid grabbing the cord. This may look cool, but can quickly lead to damaging the cord or connection. Keep your hands on the microphone neck.
5. Pull the microphone back away from your voice on high notes or during loud sections.
6. Avoid holding the mic too tight. This may cause tension in your arm, which travels to the neck and out through the mouth resonator.
7. Respect the mic by either putting it back into its stand or in its case after using it.

Good microphone technique

WRONG
Too far away.

WRONG
Too close.

CORRECT!
Note the angle.

QUICK TIPS: DO'S AND DON'TS FOR SINGERS

Stay Hydrated

Have you ever been around someone who spits when they talk? We know of one church where the first three rows are always empty. It was known by the youth group as the "spit pit."

Believe it or not, when you sing you release tiny drops of moisture with every note. Although usually unnoticeable, this involuntary process robs your vocal cords of much needed fluid. Like the engine in your car, your vocal cords need to stay lubricated during use.

What can you do about it? Drink plenty of room temperature water before you sing.

Never Spontaneously Freestyle on the Melody

This is particularly important when leading the congregation. Stay on the melody. When your singers start doing their own thing, especially if more than one improvise, you are asking for dissonance.

Never Sing with a Deadpan Face

There's a fine line between a phony smile and a joyful expression. Pray before going to the platform. Want an eye-opener? Videotape your team in action.

Never Clear Your Throat into the Microphone

Some people clear their throat without thinking. Don't do this. It only provokes the need to clear the throat even more. It is also damaging to the vocal cords. Instead, swallow a few times.

Never Yawn on Stage

Stifle it. Swallow it. Never, ever yawn. Yawning is a physiological reaction to a lack of oxygen. If you feel the need to yawn, try taking a few deep breaths.

Get That Thing out of Your Mouth

Never chew gum, eat candy, or suck on cough drops just before or during singing. Coating your throat with sweetened particles will diminish your ability to fully utilize your vocal cords.

Never Go on the Platform without Checking Your Fly

It is your spouse's worst nightmare. If you have teenagers in the congregation, it's over. There's no good way to handle it once you get in front of an audience. You can't zip it up facing the congregation. Worse yet, you can't spin around to take care of business for two reasons: One, everyone will know what you're doing. Two, if there's a choir behind you . . . well that's not an option either.

Here's how one leader handled it: "Let's bow in prayer." While the congregation had their heads down and eyes closed, he made a quick zip, and prayed, "Thank you, Lord, for the privilege of prayer. Amen."

We understand he got away with it.

When Hitting the High Notes

Open your mouth wide, drop your jaw, and try to relax your tongue and face. Avoid stretching your neck up. Air needs to come from the stomach, not the chest. It is a great idea to do a checkup from the neck up in the mirror.

No Pain. No Gain. Wrong!

Unlike your physical workout, pain is the enemy of your vocal cords. If you have pain while singing, you are doing something terribly wrong. It might be wise to go to a professional teacher (find one that also teaches contemporary singing) to get their guidance, even if it is only for a few lessons.

Stand in the Place Where You Are

Most professional vocal teachers will recommend you stand when you sing. At least, whenever you can help it. Here's why: Your voice will sound best when your torso is straight and upright (but not rigid). When you sit, some of your internal organs are slightly compressed, encumbering proper airflow.

How to Breathe

Draw air in through your mouth, not your nose, when taking breaths. Try to take air in down around your waist, not up high in your chest. This provides you with numerous benefits. First, you'll get more air. Try it now. Draw in air up high in your chest, then sing a single note until you run out of air. Then try to draw in air down low and sing the same note. If you are like most people, you will get more air and more control. Shallow chest breaths can actually make you hyperventilate. Finally, taking deep breaths can help dispel the jitters during performances.

Do I Look Fat?

Most people are a little self-conscious about the way they look when singing. Trying to hold in your stomach while singing is wrong. It is fine to do this in your swimsuit at the beach or pool, but not while performing. By sucking in your stomach, even a little bit, you not only decrease the amount of air you can take in, but you also restrict the proper airflow. If you feel your stomach sticks out too much while singing, wear loose clothes, a sport coat, or solid black—they all have a slimming effect!

Breath Control

Develop the ability to go longer and longer without taking a breath. When singing long phrases, let the air flow out gradually. While this sounds like common sense, a good exercise is to sing a sentence, then add a couple more words, then a few more. Try singing hymns or even nursery rhymes.

When to Breathe

Breathe on the punctuation marks. Never in the middle of a word! However, we have all encountered phrases where no convenient punctuation mark exists. When working on a particularly long phrase, instead of singing it, talk it through, observing where you naturally pause for a breath. Then, try singing it, taking a breath at the same place.

in CLOSing

Congratulations! You have covered plenty of ground in this chapter. Before you move on, there is one final assignment: Keeping your finger in this spot, glance back through this chapter and write yourself a reminder of several things you most want to apply. Do it right now, so you don't forget.

Things I Need to Apply from This Chapter:

1. _____ (page _____)

2. _____ (page _____)

3. _____ (page _____)

4. _____ (page _____)

5. _____ (page _____)

chapter 4

Give Your Rehearsals a Tune-Up

In This Chapter You Will Learn:

- How to prepare for rehearsals so you'll be confident.
- How to run an efficient rehearsal.
- What to do if your rehearsal is a disaster.
- Quick tips: do's and don'ts for rehearsals.

Introduction to This Chapter

If you asked a hundred praise and worship leaders which aspect of running their ministry causes the most frustration, you would likely find "running rehearsals" near the top of their lists.

The good news is you *can* run rehearsals that get results. Believe it or not, there is a way to run a rehearsal so that everyone leaves refreshed instead of exhausted, confident instead of anxious, and enthusiastic instead of apprehensive about the upcoming worship service.

In this chapter, you will learn that being prepared is the secret of conducting exceptionally smooth rehearsals. You probably already knew that. What you (like thousands of others) may have always struggled with is how to *get* prepared, which is where this chapter will help. You will learn a systematic, twelve-step method we call *prerehearsing* that will guarantee to get you prepared. Then you will learn how to handle your rehearsals the way professionals do. Pretty soon, like them, you will start getting professional results.

how to PRePaRe foR RehearsaLs so you'LL Be confiDent

When it comes to rehearsals, plenty of praise and worship leaders use one of two methods. Most simply plan or pattern their rehearsals after the ones they participated in prior to becoming a leader. Their credo: "That's the way we've always done rehearsals." Little or no thought goes into asking *what* makes rehearsals successful or *why*.

The Good news is you can Run RehearsaLs that Get ResuLts.

The second plan is worse. Someone lays out a set of songs. The group picks one and everyone dives in. At the conclusion of each song, someone declares, "Okay, that sounded good. What's next?"

The problem, of course, comes when a given song *doesn't* sound so good. There's little or no clear direction, lots of tension, and long, wearying remedies. If you have ever attended a marathon rehearsal (the kind that last until way too late in the evening), you know exactly what we mean. The problem with each is that there is plenty of "what," but little "why" or "how."

Use Our Twelve-Step Method

Hi. I'm Doug, and I'm a praise and worship leader.

Well, we won't be using a *recovery* twelve-step method, although we have met worship leaders who felt they needed one! In this next section, we will be showing you a twelve-step rehearsal preparation method that will enable you to march right into rehearsal, ready to roll.

If you want your group rehearsals to get results, you must privately prerehearse all by yourself. Here's how.

Make a Decision. Actually, Make Several

Before a worship service, there are a number of musical issues and decisions you need to make. For example, you need to choose the songs in your playlist.

Choosing the songs, however, is only the start. You also need to decide how you will arrange them for the upcoming service. You need to decide things like tempo, key changes, number of repeats, transitions, segues, song introductions, vocal arrangements (e.g., parts or unison), and more.

Unless you attend a church where everything happens spontaneously, you will make these decisions *before* the worship service. Exactly *when* before the service you make them is up to you.

We've attended rehearsals where the leader tries to make these decisions on the fly. Unfortunately, in most instances, the leaders came across looking disorganized, scattered, and undisciplined.

We recommend you make all the key decisions *before* rehearsal. That way, *during* rehearsal you look prepared, focused, and like a leader who knows where you are going. If during the actual rehearsal, you change your mind about something or feel the need to tweak anything, no problem. The choice is up to you. The success or failure of your rehearsals is largely dependent upon your preparation. People

"BUt We've aLWaYS DONe it that WaY!"

involved in discipleship ministries say you can't lead a person to a spiritual life deeper than your own. The same is true of music rehearsals—you'll sow what you reap.

Are you ready to dive into a twelve-step prerehearsal? If you're new to this level of preparing, get ready for a shock. It will feel awkward and laborious at first (most new things do). But after you've worked through the prerehearsal steps for a few weeks, you will see your rehearsals running smooth as butter. Finally, in the appendix, there's a reproducible prerehearsal checklist you can use week after week to stay on track. Let's get started.

Step 1: Pray

Really pray. If you've devolved into the habit of preceding your ministry preparation with rote, repetitive prayers where you simply use a standard generic prayer (like the one you use at meals) . . . repent.

Ask the Lord to make not only the worship service but also the rehearsal a meaningful, frustration-free experience. Pray for every member of your worship team by name, and finally pray for yourself. Ask for guidance and a clear mind as you prepare. You'll be glad you did.

Step 2: Get the Music Ready

In chapter 2 of this book, we covered arranging your music, copyright issues, creating a playlist, and using resources like printed music and chord charts. If you haven't read through that material, we suggest you stop and do it now.

When you are ready to start your private prerehearsal, you should come with your playlist in hand. Now is the time to pull the music together for everyone and put it in folders. Doing this in advance works well for several reasons. First, there's never a last-minute scramble at the photocopier, and second, there is never a delay because someone can't find their music. Since you're the leader, make it your responsibility to get all the music distributed and arranged in order.

Step 3: Confirm the Tempo for Each Song

This is usually an easy step since you gave this issue some thought as you created your playlist. It might seem silly, especially if everyone knows the songs you'll be using. However, sometimes even familiar songs don't work well back to back. What you need to do in advance is personally play through the songs in the order you've arranged them, ensuring compatible tempos.

> The success or failure of your rehearsals is largely dependent upon your preparation.

Make sure there is a clean flow from one song to the next. If there's a tempo change between songs, make sure you note it, so you can tell your players and singers what to expect, and exactly how you'll adjust the tempo between songs.

We recommend writing down the tempo somewhere on the music.

Step 4: Confirm the Instruments and Singing Arrangements for Each Song

During your arranging, you started planning how the music would be performed: singing in unison vs. parts, all instruments vs. only one, drums on the snare vs. just a rim shot, etc. Now is the time to solidify your ideas and write them down.

If you play an electronic keyboard or synthesizer, you need to choose what sounds you'll use for each song. Does this slow ballad get the electric piano or the strings? On the fast, peppy set will you use the MIDI piano or the funky one? What about the electric guitar? Clean or distortion? Reverb? Effects? Make your choices now and write them down so you don't waste time experimenting during rehearsal.

Step 5: Choose the Intro Measures

Again, even if you're doing songs that you already know, it's important to plan exactly what measures you'll use to precede the singing on each and every song.

Thankfully, some printed music already has the introduction measures included. Be careful, though. If you're linking songs together in a medley, sometimes the printed introductions are too long.

If you're not sure what measures to use for an introduction, here are two rules of thumb. The first four measures of the verse usually make good introductions. Then, the last four measures of the chorus usually work pretty well too. Experiment, but do your experimenting *before* rehearsal. You don't want to waste time stumbling around while everyone watches as you make up your mind.

> Some people like using a yellow highlighter to color the measures they'll use for the introductions.

Step 6: Play and Talk Through the Transitions, Segues, and Modulations

Now it's time to pay close attention to what happens *during* and *between* break points in your songs on your playlist. Get out your instrument and start playing and singing at the end of the first song. Plan carefully what happens next. Don't play through the whole song yet. That will come later. Focus now on the endings, beginnings, and what exactly happens between them. For example, review each of the following headings carefully and make sure you can answer each of the following questions under each.

Prepare for Transitions within Songs

If you are singing a song with multiple verses, how many beats go between the end of the chorus and the start of verse 2? Sometimes you go straight to verse 2, other times you add a measure in between. Make sure you know which for every song on your playlist.

Prepare for Segues (from One Song to the Next Song)

If you are moving from one song right into the next song, make sure *you* can play the transitions flawlessly.

- Are you using passing chords?
- What will you play between songs?

- Have you written the passing chords on the music?
- How many beats/measures does each passing chord get?

Prepare for Modulations (Changing Keys)
- If you need to change keys, what modulation chords will you use?
- How many beats or measures will you play for each modulation chord?
- Play it through to check for smoothness.

Prepare for Talking

Will you do any talking, such as providing instructions between verses or songs? If so, think about what you want to say, then go ahead and try it in advance. Yes, it feels kind of weird to talk out loud when you're all alone, but you'll find that talking it out—out loud—really has a way of working the kinks out. You will want to make sure you have enough time to fit in everything you have to say.

Congratulations, you're halfway through prerehearsal! Take a break and go get a cup of coffee.

Step 7: Review and Mark Tricky Timing

Now you want to carefully study your printed music and chord charts. It is likely your singers have heard different recording artists sing some of the songs in your playlist. Unfortunately, recording artists rarely sing music exactly as it is written. Artists always want to embellish the music and make it their own. This is fine, but guess what you get when one of your sopranos sings a song like Twila Paris and an alto sings it slightly differently, the way they did at her last church? You get cacophony.

cacophony: dissonance, confusion. You know the sound of an orchestra warming up? That's cacophony.

You need to examine the music carefully and look for areas where the timing is likely to cause people to stumble. Hymns and traditional gospel songs are written with pretty straightforward timing. Contemporary praise and worship music, however, is loaded with tricky phrases and unusual timing—that's why it sounds so cool!

Here are a few things to watch out for:

Eighth notes tied across the end of a measure. This sort of thing often distinguishes contemporary music. Make certain you can nail it.

Alternate melodies when there are a different number of syllables between two different verses. Be ready to demo each verse.

Long holds—count the beats. As you know, male singers are notorious for not holding the note for its duration.

You should mark these spots in your printed music. Be sure to practice them during your private prerehearsal until you have them down cold. During your full rehearsal, you will need to be prepared to settle debates among singers and players by insisting it be sung as written and/or as you direct.

Step 8: Identify Any Words Needing Special Pronunciation

Scan through the music again, this time paying special attention to the lyrics. In chapter 3 we pointed out typical words, phrases, or sounds that are easily mispronounced or underpronounced when sung (see page 79).

You will be helping your singers tremendously if you come to rehearsal *anticipating* these potentially troublesome sections. By identifying them in advance, you will be a step ahead and able to be proactive toward likely problems. Just before you begin a song with your singers, you might say something like, *Now watch the lyrics in verse two. Remember, "because" rhymes with "laws" not "buzz."*

We know of worship leaders who highlight tricky phrases with a pink highlighter as they prerehearse. We will cover how to actually rehearse these later in this chapter. For now you simply need to know where they are.

Step 9: Practice the Non-Melody Parts

Since you are the leader of the praise and worship team, chances are you usually sing the melodies of your songs. If you usually sing melody, it is probable that you usually ignore the other parts of the music. During your prerehearsal, make sure you can play all the parts of any song on your playlist. This is important for two reasons: First, you need to know what the *other* parts sound like so you will be able to tell if your singers are getting them right during rehearsal. Second, you need to be able to play the parts correctly and cleanly so your singers can learn them as you demonstrate.

If you are a good sight reader or you have one on your team, step 9 is usually a quick step. But don't skim by this one. We have seen plenty of worship leaders get embarrassed as they stumble and fumble, trying to pick out an alto part, especially when the timing doesn't exactly match the melody. Others are somewhat weak playing bass clef. Trying to hammer out the tenor and bass parts usually becomes a disaster for them.

To sum up, make sure you have planned where the music will be performed in unison and where it will be played in parts. Then make sure you can play the parts flawlessly for rehearsal.

Step 10: Confirm the Dynamics for Each Song in Your Playlist

Even casual musicians understand that music is more meaningful and interesting when there are dynamics. If you play four songs in a row, all at the same tempo and volume, most people will lose interest after the second one.

Evaluate and mark your music. Where do you want it to get louder? Do you want to pick up the tempo a little bit on the last verse to build anticipation? Do you plan to dramatically slow down at the end of a song?

You have thought about these things throughout your planning and prerehearsing. Right now, however, is the time to solidify your ideas and document them on the music.

Step 11: Play and Sing through the Entire Playlist

Now you get to see how all your ideas and planning comes together! To save time you can probably skip playing through multiple verses of a given song, but be sure you are comfortable with the transitions and segues. If you choose to prerehearse the entire playlist, it might be a good idea to time it. That way you will be able to see exactly how long it takes to get through the music. Adjust if you need to.

Step 12: Prepare the Final Playlist for Your Praise and Worship Team

At last! Once you have completed the previous eleven steps and you are comfortable with the way everything works, prepare a final playlist for your team. Your playlist should not only include the songs you plan to do in order, but should also contain explanatory notes about the arrangements.

We like preparing detailed playlists for several reasons:

- First, a detailed list solidifies our planning.
- Second, it gives everyone a road map to follow during rehearsal.
- Third, it makes us look really well prepared! This isn't pride; it is important because it builds confidence and enthusiasm for everyone on the team.
- Finally, team members always say how much they appreciate detailed lists. Most praise and worship team members have had their fill of leaders who wing it.

What should you include on your final playlist? We're glad you asked. We have included two sample playlists in the appendix for you to review. One is filled in, so you can see the kinds of information we suggest you to include; the second is blank so you can reproduce and use, or adapt your own from it. Don't forget there's also a blank reproducible prerehearsal checklist you might want to use to keep yourself on track. By the way, if you want to do any music education, decide what you want to cover now. Many music directors like to open rehearsals with about five minutes of music education.

One option you have is to page through the *Praise and Worship Team Instant Tune-Up!* and pull a single idea from the Quick Tips: Do's and Don'ts section of a chapter. That way, you'll have plenty of material.

One Last Step: Rehearsal Order

When you've completed your playlist, choose the order in which you'll rehearse the songs. As you'll discover in the next section, we don't necessarily recommend *starting* rehearsal with the first song on the playlist and running through them in order. Analyze all of your songs and plan to rehearse them in the following order:

1. The easiest song on the playlist
2. The next to easiest song on the playlist
3. The hardest song on the playlist
4. The next-to-hardest song on the playlist
5. Remaining songs in any order

You'll learn why this is important in the next section.

How to Run an Efficient Rehearsal

Once you have adequately and thoroughly prepared for rehearsal, it's time to rally the troops and get ready for worship. Your goal for running a rehearsal is not to fellowship. If that happens as a by-product (and it should), that's great. But remember the purpose of a rehearsal is to get ready for worship so you and your singers and players can approach the platform confidently and enthusiastically.

There are many ways to run a successful rehearsal. Your personality type probably has more to do with the atmosphere and sense of flow at your rehearsals than anything else. You no doubt are doing some things well already. But chances are, there are a few things about your rehearsals that could be improved, which is why you're reading this chapter.

Whatever your personality type, you need to recognize this: As a worship leader you are called to lead God's people into his presence. This is an extremely high calling. Don't tolerate sloppy, unfocused, undisciplined rehearsals.

To be successful you need a plan. The following ideas should help you as you develop your own rehearsal method.

Plan Your Rehearsal

Sounds obvious right? Earlier in this chapter we alluded to the way many praise and worship teams run their rehearsals:

> Start with the first song on the playlist and hammer through 'em all in order. If while playing you come across an error, pretend you didn't hear it unless the song completely falls apart. If that happens, complain briefly, then take it from the top. Soon, it will all be over and everyone gets to go home.

We are aware that many praise and worship teams do it this way, but we think there is a better way to run a rehearsal. Between here and the end of this chapter we are going to show you a rehearsal method that gets results. You can use it right now or adapt it to fit your unique situation. We will present it first in outline form, then explain each point in greater detail one at a time.

A Rehearsal Method That Gets Results!

1. Pray (3–5 minutes).

2. Explain your goals and talk through the playlist (5 minutes).

3. Rehearse the songs independently, one at a time, starting with the easiest songs.

   - Don't worry about dynamics or transitions yet.
   - Listen for and quickly correct any wrong notes, unclear enunciation, and timing errors.
   - Try hard to get through each song in 10 minutes or less. You will polish them later.

4. Next rehearse any segues and transitions between songs.

   - Don't play the whole song, start at the end, work out the transitions, and play/sing into the next song, then stop. Don't rush, but this should take only moments for each transition.

5. Take a five-minute break.

6. Replay/rehearse the entire playlist in performance order. This time focus on dynamics and flow.

Let's walk through an imaginary rehearsal, step by step, line by line.

First, Check Your Attitude

Nothing sets the tone of your rehearsal more than your attitude. You should plan to arrive early enough to set up and run your own mini sound check before everyone else. That way, as other team members arrive, you are free to greet them. Go out of your way to personally welcome *every* participant. Speak to them by name. Help them carry in their gear. If you have gotten into the habit of asking people how they are doing, make sure you have time to listen.

You need to exude a genuine sense of enthusiasm and confidence because your attitude will quickly spread like a first impression. On the other hand, if you disseminate a disposition of frustration, anxiety, and tension . . .

Start on Time

Urge your participants to arrive at rehearsal on time and ready to start. We have been to rehearsals that start a half-hour late. What a shame. If your rehearsals are scheduled to start at 7 P.M., you might encourage your players to arrive a few minutes early to set up their instruments. For example, make it a policy to arrive at 6:50 P.M.

Pray

As with your prerehearsal, flee from rote, meaningless prayer times as you start your rehearsals. Present the Lord with general requests and expect general answers. Present the Lord with specific requests and expect specific answers.

Ask God to help each singer and musician learn their music efficiently and confidently. Ask for a discerning ear as you lead, and humility as you correct. Pray that each team member will have a teachable spirit and seek only to build others up with their words, actions, and attitudes.

Should you allow team members to share personal prayer requests or keep the prayer time focused on rehearsal? While opinions vary, we recommend sharing because we believe asking about prayer requests from team members communicates an atmosphere of caring and bonding.

Review Tonight's Goals and Distribute Playlist

Right after prayer, make it clear what you want to accomplish during rehearsal. While this might seem obvious— *We want to get prepared for Sunday's service*— your team is likely to find it more helpful if you get more specific with something like this:

Tonight I want us to prepare and polish seven songs we'll be using this Sunday. One of them is a song that will be new to the congregation, so we'll need to give it a little extra attention. I'd also like to reserve about five minutes at the end of tonight's rehearsal to preview a more difficult song we'll be using two weeks from now.

Talk Through the Playlist

At this point you distribute (or refer to) your playlist. Some team leaders like to distribute printed copies, while others just write the playlist on a blackboard. Whichever way you display the playlist, you then explain *how* you plan to run tonight's rehearsal. Quickly talk through the playlist. As you do, try to incorporate as many of the following without belaboring each point:

1. Explain the atmosphere you want to create with the music you've chosen.
   We'll start this service off with "God, Your Love Is So Amazing."
   We want the congregation to feel joyous and enthusiastic, so we'll play it at a brisk tempo.

2. Note any anticipated musical difficulties.
   Notice the key change between verses 2 and 3 of this song.
   There is a tricky timing on the alto part during the chorus; we'll pay special attention to it later tonight.

3. Note special arrangements.
   On this slow ballad, we'll use only the piano until we get to the chorus.
   I want everyone to stay on the melody while the congregation learns the tune for this new song.

4. Point out any unique roles that members of your team will have.
   Judy, I want you to sing the verse of this song as a solo, the rest of the singers and the congregation will join in on the chorus.
   Rob, I want you to read this passage of Scripture as we segue from this song to the next. Plan to practice reading it out loud tonight during rehearsal.

Let's Sing and Play!

Get a Base Hit Quickly

We mentioned this earlier but it bears repeating: When we run a rehearsal, we rarely begin rehearsing the songs in performance order. We feel it is much better to start with the easiest song. Toward the end of rehearsal, you'll work through all the songs on your playlist in order, but you should plan on *starting* rehearsal with the easiest song because it enables you to launch the rehearsal with an early success. If you start with the hardest song and it flops, people are likely to get discouraged, or at least uncomfortable. A negative start is bad news for morale. Believe us, it's important to start off with a winner. Nail an easy song first since it builds confidence on the part of your band and singers, and enables everyone's voices and fingers to warm up gradually.

> Start Rehearsal with the easiest song on your playlist.

What About Vocalizing?

Some praise and worship leaders like to start rehearsals by vocalizing. We think this can be done quickly.

Here's why: Most contemporary praise and worship music is not all that challenging to singers. Let's face it, this stuff's not Handel. Also, singing the easiest song first enables everyone, not just the singers, to warm up effectively. So you end up saving precious rehearsal time. Let's get back to the first song.

Get Through the Easy Song As Confidently As You Can

While you should always listen for mistakes and errors, try your hardest to avoid correcting problems on this first song. Make mental notes of any errors you hear, but don't verbalize them yet. Instead, give plenty of praise and encouragement to everyone. You can always fix glaring problems later.

In baseball, it's important to get the first batter to first base. When this happens, it does wonders for team morale. During rehearsals, it's important to successfully get through the first song without many glitches or interruptions.

Continue Rehearsing Each Song

Move quickly to the next easiest song on your playlist. Before working through it, explain any arrangement issues, then dive in.

By the way, as you rehearse you need to learn how to multitask. You need to sing and/or play your own part(s), but you also need to listen to what everyone else is doing. Although it is impossible to apply precise percentages, it is best if the majority of your attention is on what others are doing. In other words, you need to be able to play and sing your own part so confidently, be so well prepared, that you barely have to think about it during rehearsal. Instead, you are able to focus on everyone else.

We have met choir directors, professional musicians, and worship leaders who are able to go on autopilot during rehearsals and performances. As they play and/or lead, they feel as if they enter an altered state of consciousness where they detach from concentrating on their own playing and are able to focus acutely on something else, such as worshiping or listening to others.

VOCALIZING: warming up with a variety of sung exercises (eg., do-re-mi-fa-so-la-ti-do).

The better prepared you are, the more likely it is that you'll be able to successfully multitask during rehearsals. As you rehearse the second song, listen for problems. If you hear them, don't stop in the middle of the song. Just make a mental note of where the problem happened and finish the verse/chorus. Then stop the song and fix the problem with this four-step method:

1. **Gently but clearly explain the problem.** Don't make a big deal out of the problem. Avoid singling anyone out. Simply make a clear, unambiguous statement like these:
   It sounded like we missed the timing at measure 12.
   The lyrics were a little mushy at the beginning.
   I want us to come in a little stronger at the beginning.

2. **Demonstrate the phrase correctly**. Immediately you play and/or sing it the way you want it to sound.
   Let me show you how it needs to sound.

3. **Rehearse just the problem phrase four times.** Don't start at the beginning of the song! Pick up at the start of the phrase that contained the error, play through the corrected part, then finish the phrase, but not the whole song
   Now let's try it together. Let's start at measure 15.

4. **Count off a measure and dive right in.**

Sometimes, it works better to have just the section that made the error rehearse the phrase. For example, you might say, "Just the singers" or "Just the instruments." When they do get it right, pour on the compliments. Don't do this in a phony or artificial way, but by all means show some enthusiasm when they get it right. It's contagious.

The key is to train your singers and players to fix problems quickly and efficiently. Your ability as a leader to quickly identify problems, demonstrate the correction, and walk both singers and players through it until it's corrected will dramatically enhance their respect for you and for themselves. Everyone will develop an attitude that says "Even if our team makes a mistake, we know how to fix it."

> The key is to train your players and singers to fix problems quickly and efficiently.

When your players and singers do get it right, reinforce it by repeating it several more times. Two to three additional repeats usually does the job.

Rehearse Every Segue, Every Transition

Instead of running the entire song, consider picking up at the last phrase, continue playing through the segue and into the first phrase of the next song.

Finally, Run through the Whole Playlist

Don't repeat unless there's a reason. Time it.

Using the above method might feel a little unorthodox to you and your team members who have not rehearsed this way in the past, but it enables leaders, players, and singers to enjoy an early success at rehearsal, drill down on and fix difficult phrases, nail the segues and transitions, and run through the entire playlist. If you decide to adopt this rehearsal method, be sure to enthusiastically prep your team in advance that over the next few weeks, you'll be trying a new rehearsal method you "learned about in a great new book for teams just like ours." Tell them what to expect, then execute your plan. Keep smiling, affirming success, and stay positive!

What to Do if Your Rehearsal is a Disaster

There is nothing like a disastrous rehearsal to get you on your knees. Actually, that's exactly what you should do when you have a particularly bad night. If during your rehearsal, you sense it's just not going to be a good night, quickly downshift or perhaps even shelve your playlist for another week. Pull some old standbys. It's always good to have a few good songs "on the bench." Plan to sing in unison. Plan to play it simple. Whatever you do, don't let your singers and players go home feeling like failures.

Then, after everyone leaves, pray for a miracle.

QviCK TiPS: Do'S anD Don'+S foR RehearSalS

Don't Ever Motivate with Guilt

Have you ever heard this proverb about sarcasm and mockery: "Mockery says more about the mocker than the one being mocked"?

Think about that for a minute. More often than not, we believe the same dynamic is present whenever a worship leader needs to make his team members feel guilty about their performance. Whether spontaneous or staged, public verbal assaults, temper tantrums, and crying spells rarely have a lasting effect. Actually, these types of outbursts only cause you to lose credibility. Most people see right through this sort of thing and typically write such individuals off. If you do have one or more team members who seem to be having genuine issues that are harming the productivity of the group, it is far more effective to reach that individual privately. When the whole team is assembled, it's always better to try to motivate with solid leadership (e.g., *you* are prepared), respect, and encouragement.

Just Say No to Marathon Rehearsals

Here's another proverb to ponder: "'The whippings will continue until morale improves,' said the captain to the galley slaves."

Long rehearsals typically show one thing only: an unprepared leader. This kills morale. While we have seen marathon rehearsals that double as "fellowship time" because of the freewheeling (unplanned) nature of the rehearsal, this is the exception rather than the rule.

We suggest it's better to do only a few songs well than to try to build a long but ineffective playlist. Start small if you need to when refining your rehearsal techniques, then add material later as productivity improves.

What to Do If They're Just Not Getting It

In spite of your best efforts and preparation, the sad fact is that you will encounter musical passages where someone on your team just can't get it. For example, there will be a passage that seems so simple, so obvious to you, but the bass player stumbles every time. Or the alto just can't find the right notes. What do you do?

First, you stay positive.

Here's how to teach timing, step by step:

- Clap out the rhythm.
- Sing it monotone. "Do, do, do" on rhythm.
- Sing it with the melody.

Stuck on a Transition?

If you're having trouble getting from one song to the next, stop right away. You demo the transition yourself at about half tempo. Let the players and singers "get it in their ears." The key is to start slow, then *poco a poco a tempo,* which means "little by little up to full tempo." Get it right at a much slower tempo, then gradually speed it up.

Be Brief

When making your remarks and offering corrections, try to make your explanations as short as possible. Some of us have developed the bad habit of talking too much during rehearsals.

Teaching Singers Their Parts

If you play an electronic keyboard or synthesizer, use a simple piano sound when teaching parts. A smooth, yet percussive sound is easiest to listen to. Stay away from keyboard sounds that have vibrato (i.e., flute, reed, brass, and organ sounds). You should also avoid electric piano sounds when teaching parts. Those nice, thick electric piano sounds are loaded with complex harmonics and overtones. Electric piano sounds are great when you play piano music but can be confusing to an alto trying to pick out her part.

If you're not sure how to identify electric piano sounds on your keyboard, watch for those named with words like DX, Tine, Rhodes, MIDI, Dream, and Bell. These are the most common names for electric piano sounds on modern keyboards.

When You Hit a Rough Spot in the Music

In an earlier section of the book, you learned how to prepare for rehearsals in a way that enables you to *anticipate* the trouble spots in your playlist. However, if one catches you off guard, here's what you do. Go ahead and finish that verse of the song, then stop. Don't keep going all the way through all the verses of the song, because you'll be reinforcing the error.

As you get to the end of that verse, gently say, "Okay, let's stop for just a minute. Sounds like we had a rough spot. Let's fix it together now."

Once you stop the song, go back to the section where the error occurred.

1. Explain the error you heard.
2. Demonstrate the correct way to sing or play it.
3. Then drill only that section at least four times.

We don't know how many rehearsals we've been to where a leader will correctly stop a song, point out a rough spot, demo the correct way to play or sing it, then blow it by saying, "Okay, let's take it from the top."

This is a terrible waste of time. It's far superior to start at the beginning of the problem phrase, usually no more than two or three measures before the section being repaired. Count off a measure, then play or sing from the start of the phrase, playing through the trouble spot and two measures afterward. Then stop and repeat the section at least three more times to reinforce it. Compliment everyone. Then, and only then, "Take it from the top."

Ask Your Singers to Vocalize in the Car on the Way to Rehearsal

We know professional vocal instructors will cringe at the thought of this, but you can save plenty of time by asking your singers to warm up (or at least start warming up) by singing in the car.

Consider Running Two Rehearsals

Two rehearsals?!? I have enough trouble running one! Of course you do. That's why you should consider running two. Multiple rehearsals are quite common in the world of large choirs and orchestras. In these contexts, smaller rehearsals are called *sectionals*. For example, Tuesday night might be a sectional just for the alto section. During your first rehearsal you might practice with only the musicians. Especially if you are new to leading a praise and worship ministry, running a "band only" rehearsal can really make a difference. First, it gives you a preview of what the full rehearsal is going to feel like; you get to see how your music will flow from song to song. Second, your singers will appreciate not having to wait around while the guitar player tries to learn her part.

Some like the idea of the band-only rehearsal being more casual, perhaps at your home with dinner prepared. This also provides a wonderful opportunity for bonding with your team. Other music teams run a single weekly rehearsal that lasts two hours. The first hour is a sectional, with the singers in a separate room (with their own leader) while the band stays on the platform, plugged into the PA system for their own band-only time. During the second hour, both players and singers combine for the final run-through.

Prerehearsal Checklist

Step 1: Pray.

Step 2: Get the music ready and in players' and singers' folders.

Step 3: Choose the tempo for each song.
> Play excerpts from all songs back to back to check tempo compatibility.

Step 4: Pick the instruments and arrangement for each song.

> Who plays and who sings on each verse?

Step 5: Choose the intro measures.

> How will you start each song? When do the singers come in?

Step 6: Play and talk through the transitions, segues, and modulations.
> What will you do between verses?
> What will you do between songs?
> What will you do between key changes?
> Are you using any codas?
> Are you talking between songs? Did you practice what you are going to say?

Step 7: Review and mark tricky timing.
> Where are your singers and players likely to stumble?
> Make sure you can play and sing it correctly.

Step 8: Identify any words needing special pronunciation.
> Read through the lyrics and look for:
> Words likely to be mispronounced
> Words likely to be underpronounced
> Hyphenated words
> Long notes where melody changes while holding
> Fermatas

Step 9: Practice the non-melody parts.
> Can you play or sing the alto, tenor, and bass parts?

Step 10:   Plan the dynamics for your playlist.
Where will the music change volume and/or tempo?

Step 11:   Play and sing through the entire playlist.
Final check: Did you time the music?

Step 12:   Prepare rehearsal order and notes for your praise and worship
team.

in CLOSING

Congratulations! You have covered plenty of ground in this chapter. Before you move on, there is one final assignment: Keeping your finger in this spot, glance back through this chapter and write yourself a reminder of several things you most want to apply. Do it right now, so you don't forget.

Things I Need to Apply from This Chapter:

1. _____ (page _____)

2. _____ (page _____)

3. _____ (page _____)

4. _____ (page _____)

5. _____ (page _____)

Chapter 5

Give Your Presentation a Tune-Up

In This Chapter You Will Learn:

- How to position your worship team correctly.
- How to design visual aids for maximum impact.
- How to do a sound check that will eliminate surprises.
- How to give secret signals to your sound team and band.
- How to painlessly introduce new songs to your congregation.
- Quick tips: do's and don'ts for your ministry presentation.

Introduction to This Chapter

Have you ever sat in church and had difficulty getting in sync with the worship?

Spiritual issues may sometimes be the cause of this; however, we believe more often than not that the reason people struggle to get into the worship experience is because it is poorly presented. When people can't see the lyrics to the songs, hear the worship leader, or understand their words, they tend to disengage and feel like an outsider.

You and your worship team must do everything you can to eliminate these frustrating experiences for the people in your church. This chapter is designed to help you prepare your presentation so that worship is rich and meaningful.

How to Position Your Worship Team Correctly

In this book "presentation" is what you do when in front of the congregation. Some churches call this ministering, leading, etc.

Let's begin with the way you position your worship team members on the platform. Whether you are working with nonprofessional or professional musicians and singers, it is imperative that you be able to easily and instantly communicate with each other. If something goes wrong during the service, there must be a way to get each other's attention so it can be fixed.

There is a right way and many wrong ways to arrange your team on the platform. See if you can tell the difference. Study the following diagram; then see if you can check off all the problems this team is likely to experience.

What's Wrong with This Picture?

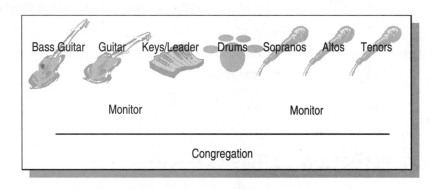

a. The instruments won't be able to see the singers.
b. The singers won't be able to see the leader.
c. The singers won't be able to see the instruments.

If you chose a, b, *and* c, you are on the right track. Positioning everyone in a straight line is hard on everyone. It is much better to create a semicircle or an inverted *V* shape (see diagram below). Each player and singer should turn and face slightly inward, at about a 45 degree angle to the congregation.

A Better Way

With this arrangement, you get the following benefits:

> Everyone can see the leader.
> Everyone can see each other.
> Everyone can see the congregation.
> The leader can give signals to the team members.

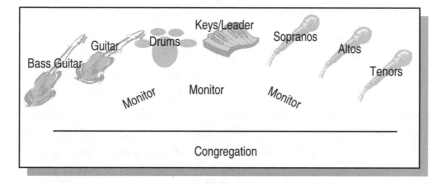

Now of course every church platform is different. In your church you may have fixed furniture such as a pulpit or choir loft to work around. Get creative. The key thing to remember is that you need to position the leader so everyone on the team can see her. It is less than ideal to put the leader out front with everyone else behind. In this arrangement, the leader needs to turn around, away from the congregation, to communicate with the team, which can be distracting.

When You're Smiling, the Whole Church Smiles with You

Get the point? You obviously don't want to plaster an artificial Miss America–style smile on your face while on the platform, but by the same token, you don't want to wear a flat expression either. One of the keys to an effective worship presentation is finding a way to generate and wear a subtle, relaxed facial expression that communicates peace and joy. You might even want to pray about it before you approach the platform.

how to Design Visual Aids for maximum impact

Three Types of Visual Aids

For all practical purposes, there are three types of visual aids you will most likely use in your ministry. Some churches like to print the song lyrics in the service bulletin or program. Others like to use overhead transparencies. Really high tech churches have computers with special projectors that display in gorgeous full color. Some churches use combinations of the above. Each has its own strengths and weaknesses. But all three can work well, provided you do each well. This section will help you evaluate and make the most of each.

Printed Lyrics (Song Sheets)

According to Christian Copyright Licensing International (CCLI), 41 percent of all churches print song lyrics in the bulletin or on a separate song sheet. Those good old song sheets sure have their benefits. To begin with, everyone who has a copy of the bulletin has the lyrics right in front of them. No one has the excuse of not being able to see the words. And there is no maintenance. After the service, they get tossed out. In our experience, though, we have found printed song sheets to be less than ideal for several reasons. First, when people use them, they are looking down, not up. Looking down while singing can cut off the windpipe, diminishing volume. Second, they waste paper, especially if the lyrics are on a separate sheet. Even in a small church, this can add up to many reams of paper over the course of a year. By the way, if you do use song sheets, get in the habit of recycling paper! Third, when holding a sheet, it makes it hard to clap or raise one's hands in praise. Finally, when looking down, some people feel cloistered, as if they are in their own little world, while looking up at a screen invokes a better sense of community and participation. If, however, you do choose to use printed lyrics, consider the following:

1. Avoid squeezing lyrics together, just to make them fit. It is much better to begin each phrase on a new line. This makes the lyrics much easier to follow.

2. Make sure you use a type size that's easy to read and large enough to read. You don't want people frustrated because they had to squint to see the lyrics, especially if you lower the sanctuary lighting during singing.

3. If you can, save the data for the typed lyrics. That way, you won't have to retype them the next time you use them. Be sure you include the copyright notices for the lyrics you use on the printed sheets. It's the law. If you need to get the scoop on copyright issues, see page 61.

4. Don't forget to use a spell checker if you produce your bulletins or song sheets with a computer. If you produce them on a typewriter, get someone to proof them.

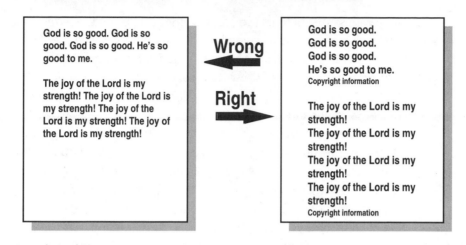

Overhead Transparencies

About 27 percent of today's churches use overhead projectors and transparencies to display lyrics. Transparencies are easy to use, easy to store, easy to read, and recyclable. If you choose to use overhead transparencies to display lyrics, consider the following:

1. Don't allow hand lettering! Not only is it hard to read, but it's often inconsistent. If you don't have a PC, someone, somewhere in your church has one. Give them a new "ministry."

2. Spread out the lyrics. If a given song has multiple verses, don't try to jam an entire song on a single transparency. The lyrics will present better if you limit each transparency to one verse and its chorus. Limiting the amount of text on each transparency also eliminates the dreaded "shifting sheet syndrome," where the sheet is slid up and down, moved, jiggled, and adjusted while on-screen, which is terribly distracting.

   Spreading out the lyrics means many of your songs will have multiple transparencies. When this is the case, it is a good idea to label each transparency with the title and number. Some people like to do this in small type at the bottom of the sheet, so it won't be noticeable or distracting to the congregation while on-screen, but it will make it easy on whoever needs to keep the transparencies organized. For example, "'As the Deer.' 1 of 3. © 1987 Hosanna's Integrity Music."

3. Make sure the printed type size is no less than 24 points. Bigger is better.

4. Use black text. Other colors are hard to read, especially from a distance. If you want to use pretty colors for borders or other art, softer tones for your artwork tend to look better than darker colors when ceiling lights are on.

5. Stay with sans serif fonts (i.e., fonts without "tails" on the letters) like Arial and Helvetica. Make sure you keep them bolded as well. Serif fonts, like Times and Garamond, are harder to read from a distance.

6. Consider getting one of those "transparency frames" that fit on the glass surface of your projector. This too will help keep the transparencies displaying straight and consistently.

7. Make sure there is always a spare light bulb in your overhead projector. By the way, if you need to change a burned-out projector bulb during worship, be careful. They get extremely hot. Also be sure to wrap the new bulb in a piece of tissue or paper so your fingers don't make contact with the glass part of the bulb. The oil on your fingers dramatically reduces the life of some types of bulbs. Here's another helpful tip: Get a piece of tissue paper, fold it neatly, and store it inside the projector near the replacement bulb (you might even tape it near the bulb). This way, when the installed bulb burns out during a service, you'll have the tissue paper needed to handle the new bulb right at your fingertips.

Computer-Generated Projection

This of course is the crème de la crème. If you can afford it, nothing looks better than presentation-software-generated lyrics, using a program such as Microsoft PowerPoint or Lotus Freelance Graphics, projected on a screen. This is how the pros do it.

While we don't have time here to help you understand all the variables in the constantly changing world of computers and projection technology, we can confidently tell you to avoid going the cheap route when it comes to buying a projector. When you do decide it's time to invest in a projector, here are a few things to keep in mind:

1. Don't believe the ads. Don't buy a projector without trying it out on site, in *your* sanctuary under actual lighting conditions. Forget everything you read in the brochures. Ignore what salespeople say on the telephone about lumens, pixels, and saturation factors. Tell the salesperson you want to see the projector in action under real-world conditions.

You might be able to negotiate renting the unit you are considering purchasing for a trial Sunday. Try to cut a deal that the rental fee gets credited toward the purchase of a new unit if you buy. If they won't let you try it before you buy it, thank them for their time, and take your business elsewhere.

Ideally, find a local projector sales representative who will bring to your church at least three or four different models, using differing technologies, qualities, and prices. Line them up side by side and turn them on one at a time. Display the same slide on each. Try out different colored backgrounds. By all means, if you plan to use your projector on Sunday mornings, run your test on a sunny morning so you get the actual room lighting conditions.

2. Don't buy a projector for the sake of buying a projector. When you run your test, be honest with yourself about what you see. If the lyrics look grainy, the colors look washed out, and the image is faint—don't buy it. It could be that your church's physical environment simply has too much light. You definitely don't want to sink several thousand dollars into a projector only to encounter murmuring among the people that they can't see the lyrics. Thankfully, new technologies are being developed right now that will bring the cost down and the quality up in the near future.

Start and End Your Presentation Right

When making your slides remember these pointers:

1. Use a blank, black screen as the first and last slide.
2. Align your text left; don't center it.
3. Keep the text big. Use a bold, sans serif font. PC fonts such as Arial Black, Helvetica, and Tahoma look best when projected.
4. Don't use all capital letters. They are harder to read.
5. With computer projectors, it almost always looks best to use a light text on a dark background.
6. On the last slide of each song, include some sort of small but noticeable visual cue, so the person changing the slides knows when you have reached the last slide of a given song. For example, you might place a small red box in the lower right corner. This way they can pause, waiting for your verbal or musical cue to move on to the next song. This will spare them the embarrassment of prematurely jumping to the next song.

Now that your team is correctly positioned on the platform and your visuals are ready, you are almost ready to begin. Before you do though, don't neglect the next critical step.

How to Do A Sound Check That Will Eliminate Surprises

You have probably seen people get up in front of the church, begin to speak into the microphone, and you hear . . . nothing. Then the person working the sound system panics, quickly increases the volume, and blasts everyone out of their pews.

The potential for this problem increases exponentially as you add instruments and singers. The good news is you can prevent it by running a quick and efficient sound check. Here is a systematic method that usually takes less than five minutes.

Get Up. Get Done. Get Down.

Make sure your worship team and sound system crew understand you want to get up, finish the sound check, and get off the platform quickly and inconspicuously. Your sound check should work like a quick and quiet drill, not a last minute rehearsal.

Get your team—players and singers—in place on the platform. Make a rule: No talking or goofing off during the sound check. Everyone needs to be paying attention and *listening*. Your sound system/audio technicians (sound techs) should be at the sound system, paying close attention to you. Work through these steps in order:

YOUR SOUND CHECK ShOULD WORK LiKe a QUICK anD QUieT DRILL, noT a LaST minUTe ReheaRSaL.

Step 1: House Speakers Down/Off, Monitors Up

The first thing you are going to do is make sure your singers and players can hear themselves in the monitors. Begin by asking your sound techs to turn the house speakers down or off. This should be done for two reasons. First, your singers and players need to listen to themselves in the monitors, not the house system. Second, you don't want your entire sound check amplified throughout the sanctuary. That, my friends, is cheesy.

Step 2: Individual Singers at the Mics

Now, one by one, ask your singers if they can hear themselves in the monitors. One by one, get your singers to *sing* a phrase. For goodness sake, get away from the "Check 1–2–3" routine! Nobody says "Check 1–2–3" during a worship service, so why would you use that phrase for a sound check? Since you will be singing during the service, you need to sing during the sound check. Isn't that common sense? If your singers feel embarrassed or say, "I don't know what to sing," feed them a line like "Amazing Grace" or "Happy Birthday."

This is important: Make sure your singers don't lean into the mic as they sing their sound check. Have you ever noticed singers doing this? Whether they hold the mic or place it in a stand, when it is their turn some people drop their chin, lean into the mic, and say, "Check. Check 1–2–3."

Watch your singers and don't let them do this! During the sound check their mouth needs to be the same distance from the mic as it will be during the service.

Listen to each singer, one at a time. Talk to your sound techs and adjust the volume if you need to. Make sure your singers can hear themselves in the monitors.

Step 3: All Singers Singing At Once

Now, ask your singers if they can hear themselves in the monitors when everyone else is singing.

Count off a measure and get all your singers to sing a phrase from the morning's music *a capella*. Make sure they can hear themselves clearly. It is important that your singers can hear themselves. If they can't, it's easy for their voices to drift sharp or flat. Hearing themselves in the monitors really helps keep them on pitch.

Step 4: Individual Players at Their Instruments

Now it's time to work with your players. Gently remind your singers that there's to be no talking. Get each instrumentalist to play a few measures all by themselves. Like the sound check for the singers, you ask each player if they can hear himself in the monitor.

Step 5: All Players Playing at Once

Count off a measure and get the whole band to play at once. A few bars should suffice. Here you want to make sure there is a good balance among all instruments—with no one drowning out anyone else. Ask your players if they can hear themselves when everyone is playing.

Step 6: All Players and All Singers at Once, Then the House

Now, get your playlist for today's music. Pick a phrase from a slow song and another from a fast song. All sing and play a few bars of the slow one, then quickly switch to a few bars from the fast song. At this point you need to listen to the blend in the monitors. When you are satisfied with the blend and balance in the monitors, instruct your sound tech to gradually turn up and adjust the house speakers as you repeat the phrase from the slow song, then the phrase from the fast one.

Thank everyone. Then get off the platform. Remind your sound techs to watch you closely during the first set of songs for hand signals. We will learn about hand signals later in this chapter.

Don't Touch That Dial!

Once your sound check is complete, insist that your sound techs leave the controls alone. Some sound techs have a hard time with the temptation to continually tweak, fiddle, and piddle with all those exciting knobs on the sound mixer. When you allow this to happen, you are asking for trouble. Adjustments to the sound system should never be made unless the microphones and instruments are in use.

In the appendix of this book there is an abbreviated sound check chart you might want to photocopy and tape to your mixer. That way, whoever is running sound will know what to expect.

how +o Give Secre+ SiGnalS +o youR SounD Team

Maybe you never realized it, but when you watch professional praise and worship leaders, they communicate with their sound techs throughout their presentation.

How do they do it? Like baseball pitchers and their catchers, they use a discreet system of hand signals—like a kind of professional sign language. Think about it. Which is better? During a worship service, you suddenly yell out to your sound tech: "Hey, Jerry! I can't hear myself in the monitor!" or to communicate with Jerry with an almost secret hand signal that no one notices? With the former, the whole congregation is distracted, Jerry is possibly embarrassed, and you lose your concentration. With the hand signal, you are smooth as silk.

Yes, you and your sound techs need to learn a few of these signals. Let's see how they work.

When it comes to the people running your sound system, you will really only need to say four things:

1. "Turn my microphone up. I can't hear myself."
2. "Turn my microphone down. I'm too loud."
3. "Turn my instrument up. I can't hear it."
4. "Turn my instrument down. It's too loud."

Rather than making a public statement, it is much better to use subtle, secret hand signals.

Referring to Your Instrument

If you point your index finger up, as if you were making the number 1, it also looks like the letter *I*. Let your sound techs know that whenever you hold up your index finger, you want to adjust the volume of your instrument. In other words *I* stands for "my instrument."

Immediately after you hold up your index finger, you can quickly use the thumb up or thumb down gesture to indicate which direction you need the volume to go in your monitor. You should be able to quickly display this signal, just like a baseball catcher signaling the pitcher, then get back to the business of playing.

If you play keyboards, you can quickly learn and use this signal with your left hand, so you can hold chords with your right. Guitarists, it is just the opposite, flash the signal with your right hand.

Naturally, you must train your sound techs to constantly scan the worship team, watching for signals. You might need to help them unlearn bad habits of "setting and forgetting" the sound system.

Referring to Your Voice or Microphone

Holding up two fingers (like a peace sign) also kind of looks like the letter *V*. Let your sound techs know that whenever you hold up your index and middle fingers, you want to adjust the volume of your microphone. In other words *V* stands for "my voice."

Just as with the *I* signal, you can quickly flourish the *V*, then thumb up/down to let the person at the mixer know to turn your microphone up or to turn it down.

By the way, make sure your sound tech knows that your signals refer only to the volume in the monitors. It is unlikely that while you are on the platform you'll be able to hear much of what's going on in the house. You will need to trust your sound people to get the right mix there.

One way to make sure they are getting it right is to connect a tape recorder to the mixer and record an actual worship service. Then, sometime when the church is empty, play the tape back through the sound system. The dynamics are of course a little different in an empty sanctuary, but this will still give you a pretty good idea of what the congregation is hearing.

How to Give Secret Signals to Your Band

There will be times when you want to quickly and subtly communicate to your team members up on the stage with you. Train your players and singers to glance at you during the transitions on your playlist. They shouldn't stop and stare at you, but naturally glance at you, ready to receive instructions. For most worship teams, three signals will suffice.

Take It from the Top

You are on stage, the congregation is enthusiastic about your ministry, and you feel the need to repeat that song. Before you say anything to the congregation, give your band and singers a signal. Point your index finger up and move your hand in a small horizontal circular motion—as if you were twirling your hair around your fingertip. During rehearsal remind them that this signal means repeat from the beginning of the singing part, not the song introduction.

Take It from the Chorus

When you decide you want to repeat just the chorus, give your teammates a similar signal, but this time, you *point* down as you rotate your hand, as if you were running your forefinger around the rim of a glass.

We're About to End This Song

As you know, all good things must come to an end. To tell your band and singers you want to stop, give them a signal of a closed fist. It's best to provide this signal about halfway through the final chorus, so they have a clear idea where you're headed. By the way, the universally recognized signal for "cut"—a finger drawn slowly across the throat—doesn't look very good on stage, especially while playing and singing worship music. So don't signal your band to close out a song by mimicking a decapitation! Stay with the closed fist.

How to Painlessly Introduce New Songs to Your Congregation

Many praise and worship leaders experience terrible frustration when trying to introduce new music to their church. Instead of finding an enthusiastic group of people heartily joining in, they are often faced with a sea of skeptical, tight-lipped faces. The good news is there is a method you can use to maximize your people's ability to catch on and enjoy new music. Other praise and worship leaders do it, and you can too. We are going to share with you the secret the pros use to get people singing quickly, easily, and enthusiastically.

Make the Lyrics Clear

We already covered this earlier, but it bears repeating here. If your people can't see the lyrics clearly, don't expect them to sing out.

Before You Teach, Plant the Seed

Begin introducing the new music, especially the melody, before you want people to start singing it. Your goal is to plant it in their subconscious! Here are a few ideas to get you started.

Play It before You Want Your People to Sing It

If you play recorded music over the sound system as people enter the sanctuary, make sure the new song is on the tape twice. Once near the beginning of the tape and once at the end—so the song is the last piece they hear before the service starts.

Perform It before You Want Your People to Sing It

Sing your new song as a solo the week before you teach it to the church. You can do this as a special presentation soloist song or in your praise and worship medley. Either way, sing it first without the congregation.

Play the Song during Other Parts of the Service

Play the song as a prelude, offertory, postlude, or during any other "filler opportunity" in the service. For lack of a better term, churches use "filler music" all over the place (or they should). Consider these examples:

- During the greeting segment of the service
- Soft music played during prayer times
- While the bread and cup are being distributed during communion
- Between testimonies and congregational interaction, when someone is walking from their seat to the platform, etc.

The key is to use every opportunity to get the melody into your people's heads and hearts.

How to Teach So They Will Learn

Follow this arrangement and we guarantee your people will be singing along before you know it.

1. As always, it is important that you be enthusiastic (but not giddy) about the new music. You need to smile and be confident as you teach.
2. Explain why you chose this song, how you came across the song, why you want your people to learn it, or how it fits today's theme—playing the tune

in the background as you speak. Be brief. People don't need a five-minute explanation. Tell them you want them to listen as your team sings through the chorus once, then you will invite them to join in.

3. Start by having your praise and worship team sing the chorus accompanied by one instrument only (preferably guitar or keys).

It is important that everyone on the team sing in unison (all singing the melody). Make sure your singers make eye contact with the congregation and smile! As the last phrase of the chorus is sung by your team, talk on top of the music, saying something like this: "Okay, now you try singing with us."

Make sure you stop singing and start talking during the last two measures, not in between the last measure and the first. People need more warning.

4. Give a clear nod to the congregation on the downbeat and repeat the same chorus. This time, your other instruments should join in. Praise and worship singers should continue to sing in unison.

PeoPLe Don't need a five-minute exPLanation.

The added instruments should give the song additional tonal body, which really encourages everyone, because when combined with the singing, it really fills up the sound. Like before, as the last phrase of the chorus is sung by your team, talk on top of the music, saying something like this: "You did great! Now just listen as we show you how the verse goes."

Make sure you stop singing and start talking during the last two measures, *not* in between the last measure and the first. If you are like most of us, you will need to practice this privately and then rehearse it with your team.

5. All instruments continue playing and your whole worship team sings the verse in unison. Be sure you make eye contact and smile! If you look tense, your people will reciprocate. As the last phrase of the verse is sung by your team, talk on top of the music and invite your congregation to repeat the chorus.

6. This time through the chorus, your singers get to sing parts. This makes your sound even bigger. With the added confidence of having gone through it once before, your people should sing with increased vigor. If you can, pick up the tempo just a bit. Not too much—just a tiny bit. This also gives the

song a sense of build and lift. At the last phrase, talk on top of the music and say something like this: "Sounds wonderful! Try the verse with us."

7. Repeat the verse. If your song has multiple verses, use the first verse again. This time, your team members sing parts to keep the sound big. At the last phrase, you need to do two things, encourage and warn. Say something like this: "I see you've got it now. Let's take it up a notch."

8. Repeat the chorus but modulate to a new key.

There's a chart in the appendix of this book that shows you how to change keys (page 137). All instruments play, and singers sing parts. Pick up the tempo again, then complete the song. Don't forget to thank your congregation for their willingness to participate.

QUICK TIPS: DO'S AND DON'TS FOR YOUR MINISTRY PRESENTATION

Never Apologize for Not Being Prepared

Good morning everyone! We didn't get a chance to rehearse this week, but here goes . . .

What a terrible way to start ministry! You might as well say, "Good morning everyone! Let's begin worship on a negative note as we bring less than our best to the Lord."

When you were in school, did you ever pray right before an exam, asking God to help you do well in spite of the fact that you didn't study? What happened? If you didn't adequately prepare for worship, we recommend you first privately ask God's forgiveness, then ask him to help you do well in spite of your lack of diligence. He *always* forgives and *often* helps us do better than we deserve, doesn't he?

Next, get up on the platform and start leading worship as if you did prepare. Don't apologize in advance, because you haven't done a poor job yet.

Pay Attention Here

If you apologize before you present, you lose either way. If God grants you mercy and you present well, you lose credibility as people think: *What was he talking about? I thought the worship was fine.*

If you do happen to play and sing poorly, you reinforce the fact that you failed to prepare. If you say nothing, then blow it, at least some people are likely to feel sorry for you and pray for you. It's better to get up and give it your best shot. Avoid fancy stuff. Provide clear instructions.

And finally, don't let it happen again.

Prepare What You're Going to Say between Songs

Spontaneity can be a good thing. It *can* be. More often than not, unless you are particularly gifted in extemporaneous speech, not planning ahead ends up sounding . . . well . . . as if you didn't plan ahead.

You don't need to script your transitions out word for word, but do yourself a favor and privately practice what you'll say. If you stumble over your words, thank the Lord for helping you work out the kinks *before* you're in front of the church.

Never Tell Inside Jokes While on the Platform

Maybe you had a great time at the church camping trip. It was hilarious when Bob fell out of the fishing boat. For the rest of the weekend, a few of you nicknamed Bob "Soggy." It was hysterical. Now, it is Sunday at church. When you see Bob in the congregation, you call him by his new nickname. A few people snicker, but everyone else is left in the dark. This makes people feel alienated and disconnected.

Always Do a Sound Check before Going on the Platform

We've seen it happen more than once. Everyone is in a hurry. Sunday school dismissed late. The players grab their instruments, plug in, and start playing. Then, after a few measures, everyone realizes the bass's A string is horribly out of tune. Or the keyboard player suddenly discovers that instead of her favorite piano patch, her keyboard was set inadvertently to "Martian Spaceship." Professionals don't start without a sound check. Neither should you.

Never Talk to the Sound or Light Helpers in a Sarcastic Tone of Voice

Hey, Jimmy. We'd like to hear ourselves in the monitors if it's okay with you. Sheesh.

During a service, you should avoid *talking* to your techs altogether. It is much better to use the hand signals. If you do need to communicate, no matter how frustrated you are, "do not let any unwholesome talk come out of your mouths" (Ephesians 4:29).

Never Lead Worship with Sin in Your Heart

The psalmist asks: "Who may ascend the hill of the Lord? Who may stand in his holy place?"

And then answers: "He who has clean hands and a pure heart" (Psalm 24:3–4).

If you want to be used mightily by God, do all you can to make sure you're right with others and with God.

Never Embarrass Other Team Members, Especially in Front of the Church

Sally was a little flat on that last number. Sally, can you sharpen up a little? Can someone get Sally a little coffee?

We have seen worship leaders try to be funny at the expense of other team members. Bad idea. Even if it does get a laugh, it sets a poor example, especially for children in the congregation.

We think it's far better to cover for team members when they make mistakes. Remember the words of Solomon: "Love covers over all wrongs" (Proverbs 10:12).

Don't Talk in a Phony Voice

Maybe it's a generational thing, but we have always been mystified by preachers who have a unique "preaching voice" and a regular, daily conversational voice. Perhaps you've been around others who have their everyday voice, but also have a special "prayer voice" that's characterized by unnatural phrasing and variations in pitch or a sudden transformation to King James English.

In the same way, we are stymied when we hear worship leaders talk as if they are addressing a group of puppies instead of adults. In some Christian circles, when a leader hits the stage, they begin using a voice that sounds like they've suddenly become a radio announcer or a game show host. Is there a good reason why you can't just be yourself?

Dead Air Is the Enemy: Get Rid of It

In the radio and television broadcast industries, it's important to always have *something* going out over the airwaves. That's why, for example, when you listen to a song on the radio, the nanosecond it's over, one of three things happens:

1. Another song starts
2. The DJ starts talking
3. A commercial starts

People in broadcasting will tell you it's imperative to avoid dead air—gaps of silence in the broadcast. Why? Because dead air causes people to disengage, lose interest, or, heaven forbid, switch stations. It is amazing how just a few seconds of dead air can translate into boredom.

The same thing often happens in church. Dead air causes many people to disengage from worship. Make sure that as you plan your worship, you always have something going on. As covered more fully elsewhere in this book, at the end of a song you can:

1. Create a musical segue that flows right into the next song, without stopping your playing
2. Start talking while playing a segue
3. Ask the congregation to applaud, bow for prayer, stand, sit, greet one another, etc.
4. Immediately introduce the next event in the service

The Best Way to Immediately Revolutionize Your Team's Presentation

Videotape your team in action. Watch the video alone, then invite your team over for popcorn to watch. People will be shocked when they see themselves wearing deadpan faces, scratching an itch, allowing their eyes to wander around the room. During your debriefing, don't be too critical. Point out the problems, but avoid embarrassing your team members. Which is better?

This?

From the congregation's viewpoint, it looks best if team members look at the soloist when he's singing. Let's make it our goal to look where we want the congregation to look.

Or this?

Now watch as Sally blows it here by looking at the ceiling instead of the soloist! Hey Sally, what's going on up there on the ceiling?

Don't Talk Too Much

Some worship leaders feel "led" to preach mini-sermons between songs. While we are sure you have plenty to say, most people respond better to a stream of skillfully blended songs. If you must talk, keep your comments brief and vamp (improvise on your instrument) while you talk. Make it your goal to avoid the abrupt start-stop-start-stop flow that makes worship choppy.

Avoid Using Musical and Other Symbols on Your Visual Aids

Whether you use song sheets, overhead transparencies, or computer-generated images, don't use the repeat symbol (:‖) or "2X" on visual aids the congregation will see to indicate something should be done twice. It is much better to clearly label the verse and chorus and place instructions in parentheses like this:

Chorus:
Amazing love, how can it be,
That thou, my God, shouldst die for me?" (To verse)

Resist Letting Your Eyes Wander All Over the Sanctuary

Have you ever seen someone on the platform do this? First, they are looking at their feet, then gazing up at the ceiling, then trying to find their friends in the congregation. From the audience's perspective, it looks like they are not paying attention (and they probably aren't!).

They don't have to *stare* at the person talking or soloing, but they should avoid wandering eyes. Tell your singers and players to look wherever the congregation should be looking.

in closing

Congratulations! You have covered plenty of ground in this chapter. Before you close the book, there is one final assignment: Keeping your finger in this spot, glance back through this chapter and write yourself a reminder of several things you most want to apply. Do it right now, so you don't forget.

Things I Need to Apply from This Chapter:

1. _____ (page _____)
2. _____ (page _____)
3. _____ (page _____)
4. _____ (page _____)
5. _____ (page _____)

APPENDIX

WORSHIP PLANNING RESOURCES

This appendix is a bonus component of *The Praise and Worship Team Instant Tune-Up*. Excited? We knew you would be.

This section includes a number of resources we think you'll find useful as you apply the ideas and strategies outlined throughout this book. Some are worksheets designed for you to use during your personal planning sessions. Others are reproducible sheets you might want to use week in, week out, and distribute to your team members as you plan your worship services. Inside you'll find:

- **A modulation chart for all keys**
- **A guitar chords capo chart**
- **A song screening worksheet**
- **A completed sample and a blank playlist**
- **A prerehearsal checklist**
- **A blank rehearsal planner**
- **A sound check planner**

modulation chart

This chart will give you a ready-to-use set of modulation measures you can use whenever you need to modulate.

How to use this chart:

1. In the left column, find your original key and the key you wish to modulate to.
2. Try the chords in the modulation measures listed in the successive columns.

You can use this chart in three ways:

1. Play transition chord 1 for half a measure, then transition chord 2 for the other half.
2. Skip transition chord 1 and play transition chord 2 for a full measure.
3. Play the alternates in square brackets, one measure each.

Key of C Moving from:	(Old root) 1st song ending:	(Trans. Chd. 1) then play this:	(Trans. Chd. 2) then this:	(New root) then the new song/key:
C to D♭	C	G♭ [alt E♭m7]	A♭7 [alt G♭/A♭]	D♭
C to D	C	G [alt Em7]	A7 [alt G/A]	D
C to E♭	C	A♭ [alt Fm7]	B♭7 [alt A♭/B♭]	E♭
C to E	C	A [alt F#m7]	B7 [alt A/B]	E
C to F	C	B♭ [alt Gm7]	C7 [alt B♭/C]	F
C to F#	C	B [alt G#m7]	C#7 [alt B/C#]	F#
C to G	C	C [alt Am7]	D7 [alt C/D]	G
C to A♭	C	D♭ [alt B♭m7]	E♭7 [alt D♭/E♭]	A♭
C to A	C	D [alt Bm7]	E7 [alt D/E]	A
C to B♭	C	E♭ [alt Cm7]	F7 [alt E♭/F]	B♭
C to B	C	E [alt C#m7]	F#7 [alt E/F#]	B

Key of D♭

Moving from:	(Old root) 1st song ending:	(Trans. Chd. 1) then play this:	(Trans. Chd. 2) then this:	(New root) then the new song/key:
D♭ to D	D♭	G [alt F#m7]	A7 [alt G/A]	D
D♭ to E♭	D♭	A♭ [alt Fm7]	B♭7 [alt A♭/B♭]	E♭
D♭ to E	D♭	A [alt F#m7]	B7 [alt A/B]	E
D♭ to F	D♭	B♭ [alt Gm7]	C7 [alt B♭/C]	F
D♭ to G♭	D♭	B [alt A♭m7]	D♭7 [alt B/D♭]	G♭
D♭ to G	D♭	C [alt Am7]	D7 [alt C/D]	G
D♭ to A♭	D♭	D♭ [alt B♭m7]	E♭7 [alt D♭/E♭]	A♭
D♭ to A	D♭	D [alt Bm7]	E7 [alt D/E]	A
D♭ to B♭	D♭	C [alt Cm7]	F7 [alt E♭/F]	B♭
D♭ to B	D♭	E [alt C#m7]	F#7 [alt E/F#]	B
D♭ to C	D♭	F [alt Dm7]	G7 [alt F/G]	C

Key of E♭

Moving from:	(Old root) 1st song ending:	(Trans. Chd. 1) then play this:	(Trans. Chd. 2) then this:	(New root) then the new song/key:
E♭ to E	E♭	A [alt F#m7]	B7 [alt A/B]	E
E♭ to F	E♭	B♭ [alt Gm7]	C7 [alt B♭/C]	F
E♭ to G♭	E♭	B [alt A♭m7]	D♭7 [alt B/D♭]	G♭
E♭ to G	E♭	C [alt Am7]	D7 [alt C/D]	G
E♭ to A♭	E♭	D♭ [alt B♭m7]	E♭7 [alt D♭/E♭]	A♭
E♭ to A	E♭	D [alt Bm7]	E7 [alt D/E]	A
E♭ to B♭	E♭	C [alt Cm7]	F7 [alt E♭/F]	B♭
E♭ to B	E♭	E [alt C#m7]	F#7 [alt E/F#]	B
E♭ to C	E♭	F [alt Dm7]	G7 [alt F/G]	C
E♭ to D♭	E♭	G♭ [alt E♭m7]	A♭7 [alt G♭/A♭]	D♭
E♭ to D	E♭	G [alt Em7]	A [alt G/A]	D

Key of E

Moving from:	(Old root) 1st song ending:	(Trans. Chd. 1) then play this:	(Trans. Chd. 2) then this:	(New root) then the new song/key:
E to F	E	Bb [alt Gm7]	C7 [alt Bb/C]	F
E to F#	E	B [alt G#m7]	Db7 [alt B/C#]	F#
E to G	E	C [alt Am7]	D7 [alt C/D]	G
E to Ab	E	Db [alt Bbm7]	Eb7 [alt Db/Eb]	Ab
E to A	E	D [alt Bm7]	E7 [alt D/E]	A
E to Bb	E	C [alt Cm7]	F7 [alt Eb/F]	Bb
E to B	E	E [alt C#m7]	F#7 [alt E/F#]	B
E to C	E	F [alt Dm7]	G7 [alt F/G]	C
E to Db	E	Gb [alt Ebm7]	Ab7 [alt Gb/Ab]	Db
E to D	E	G [alt Em7]	A [alt G/A]	D
E to Eb	E	Ab [alt Fm7]	Bb7 [alt Ab/Bb]	Eb

Key of F

Moving from:	(Old root) 1st song ending:	(Trans. Chd. 1) then play this:	(Trans. Chd. 2) then this:	(New root) then the new song/key:
F to F#	F	B [alt Abm7]	Db7 [alt B/Db]	F#
F to G	F	C [all Am7]	D7 [alt C/D]	G
F to Ab	F	Db [alt Bbm7]	Eb7 [alt Db/Eb]	Ab
F to A	F	D [alt Bm7]	E7 [alt D/E]	A
F to Bb	F	C [alt Cm7]	F7 [alt Eb/F]	Bb
F to B	F	E [alt C#m7]	F#7 [alt E/F#]	B
F to C	F	F [alt Dm7]	G7 [alt F/G]	C
F to Db	F	Gb [alt Ebm7]	Ab7 [alt Gb/Ab]	Db
F to D	F	G [alt Em7]	A [alt G/A]	D
F to Eb	F	Ab [alt Fm7]	Bb7 [alt Ab/Bb]	Eb
F to E	F	A [alt F#m7]	B7 [alt A/B]	E

Key of F♯

Moving from:	(Old root) 1st song ending:	(Trans. Chd. 1) then play this:	(Trans. Chd. 2) then this:	(New root) then the new song/key:
F♯ to G	F♯	C [alt Am7]	D7 [alt C/D]	G
F♯ to A♭	F♯	D♭ [alt B♭m7]	E♭7 [alt D♭/E♭]	A♭
F♯ to A	F♯	D [alt Bm7]	E7 [alt D/E]	A
F♯ to B♭	F♯	C [alt Cm7]	F7 [alt E♭/F]	B♭
F♯ to B	F♯	E [alt C♯m7]	F♯7 [alt E/F♯]	B
F♯ to C	F♯	F [alt Dm7]	G7 [alt F/G]	C
F♯ to D♭	F♯	G♭ [alt E♭m7]	A♭7 [alt G♭/A♭]	D♭
F♯ to D	F♯	G [alt Em7]	A [alt G/A]	D
F♯ to E♭	F♯	A♭ [alt Fm7]	B♭7 [alt A♭/B♭]	E♭
F♯ to E	F♯	A [alt F♯m7]	B7 [alt A/B]	E
F♯ to F	F♯	A♯ [alt Gm7]	C7 [alt B♭/C]	F

Key of G

Moving from:	(Old root) 1st song ending:	(Trans. Chd. 1) then play this:	(Trans. Chd. 2) then this:	(New root) then the new song/key:
G to A♭	G	D♭ [alt B♭m7]	E♭7 [alt D♭/E♭]	A♭
G to A	G	D [alt Bm7]	E7 [alt D/E]	A
G to B♭	G	C [alt Cm7]	F7 [alt E♭/F]	B♭
G to B	G	E [alt C♯m7]	F♯7 [alt E/F♯]	B
G to C	G	F [alt Dm7]	G7 [alt F/G]	C
G to D♭	G	G♭ [alt E♭m7]	A♭7 [alt G♭/A♭]	D♭
G to D	G	G [alt Em7]	A [alt G/A]	D
G to E♭	G	A♭ [alt Fm7]	B♭7 [alt A♭/B♭]	E♭
G to E	G	A [alt F♯m7]	B7 [alt A/B]	E
G to F	G	A♯ [alt Gm7]	C7 [alt B♭/C]	F
G to F♯	G	B [alt G♯m7]	C♯7 [alt B/C♯]	F♯

Key of A♭

Moving from:	(Old root) 1st song ending:	(Trans. Chd. 1) then play this:	(Trans. Chd. 2) then this:	(New root) then the new song/key:
A♭ to A	A♭	D [alt Bm7]	E7 [alt D/E]	A
A♭ to B♭	A♭	C [alt Cm7]	F7 [alt E♭/F]	B♭
A♭ to B	A♭	E [alt C#m7]	F#7 [alt E/F#]	B
A♭ to C	A♭	F [alt Dm7]	G7 [alt F/G]	C
A♭ to D♭	A♭	G♭ [alt E♭m7]	A♭7 [alt G♭/A♭]	D♭
A♭ to D	A♭	G [alt Em7]	A [alt G/A]	D
A♭ to E♭	A♭	A♭ [alt Fm7]	B♭7 [alt A♭/B♭]	E♭
A♭ to E	A♭	A [alt F#m7]	B7 [alt A/B]	E
A♭ to F	A♭	A# [alt Gm7]	C7 [alt B♭/C]	F
A♭ to F#	A♭	B [alt G#m7]	C#7 [alt B/C#]	F#
A♭ to G	A♭	C [alt Am7]	D7 [alt C/D]	G

Key of A

Moving from:	(Old root) 1st song ending:	(Trans. Chd. 1) then play this:	(Trans. Chd. 2) then this:	(New root) then the new song/key:
A to B♭	A	C [alt Cm7]	F7 [alt E♭/F]	B♭
A to B	A	E [alt C#m7]	F#7 [alt E/F#]	B
A to C	A	F [alt Dm7]	G7 [alt F/G]	C
A to D♭	A	G♭ [alt E♭m7]	A♭7 [alt G♭/A♭]	D♭
A to D	A	G [alt Em7]	A [alt G/A]	D
A to E♭	A	A♭ [alt Fm7]	B♭7 [alt A♭/B♭]	E♭
A to E	A	A [alt F#m7]	B7 [alt A/B]	E
A to F	A	A# [alt Gm7]	C7 [alt B♭/C]	F
A to F#	A	B [alt G#m7]	C#7 [alt B/C#]	F#
A to G	A	C [alt Am7]	D7 [alt C/D]	G
A to A♭	A	D♭ [alt B♭m7]	E♭7 [alt D♭/E♭]	A♭

Key of B♭

Moving from:	(Old root) 1st song ending:	(Trans. Chd. 1) then play this:	(Trans. Chd. 2) then this:	(New root) then the new song/key:
B♭ to B	B♭	E [alt C#m7]	F#7 [alt E/F#]	B
B♭ to C	B♭	F [alt Dm7]	G7 [alt F/G]	C
B♭ to D♭	B♭	G♭ [alt E♭m7]	A♭7 [alt G♭/A♭]	D♭
B♭ to D	B♭	G [alt Em7]	A [alt G/A]	D
B♭ to E♭	B♭	A♭ [alt Fm7]	B♭7 [alt A♭/B♭]	E♭
B♭ to E	B♭	A [alt F#m7]	B7 [alt A/B]	E
B♭ to F	B♭	A# [alt Gm7]	C7 [alt B♭/C]	F
B♭ to F#	B♭	B [alt G#m7]	C#7 [alt B/C#]	F#
B♭ to G	B♭	C [alt Am7]	D7 [alt C/D]	G
B♭ to A♭	B♭	D♭ [alt B♭m7]	E♭7 [alt D♭/E♭]	A♭
B♭ to A	B♭	D [alt Bm7]	E7 [alt D/E]	A

Key of B

Moving from:	(Old root) 1st song ending:	(Trans. Chd. 1) then play this:	(Trans. Chd. 2) then this:	(New root) then the new song/key:
B to C	B	F [alt Dm7]	G7 [alt F/G]	C
B to D♭	B	G♭ [alt E♭m7]	A♭7 [alt G♭/A♭]	D♭
B to D	B	G [alt Em7]	A [alt G/A]	D
B to E♭	B	A♭ [alt Fm7]	B♭7 [alt A♭/B♭]	E♭
B to E	B	A [alt F#m7]	B7 [alt A/B]	E
B to F	B	A# [alt Gm7]	C7 [alt B♭/C]	F
B to F#	B	B [alt G#m7]	C#7 [alt B/C#]	F#
B to G	B	C [alt Am7]	D7 [alt C/D]	G
B to A♭	B	D♭ [alt B♭m7]	E♭7 [alt D♭/E♭]	A♭
B to A	B	D [alt Bm7]	E7 [alt D/E]	A
B to B♭	B	E♭ [alt Cm7]	F7 [alt E♭/F]	B♭

GUITAR TRANSPOSER
Guitar Chords Capo Chart

Need to play in an unfamiliar key?
Try using a capo. This chart will help.

When you play this	Placing capo@1 makes	Placing capo@2 makes	Placing capo@3 makes	Placing capo@4 makes	Placing capo@5 makes	Placing capo@6 makes	Placing capo@7 makes
C	C#/Db	D	D#/Eb	E	F	F#/Gb	G
C#/Db	D	D#/Eb	E	F	F#/Gb	G	G#/Ab
D	D#/Eb	E	F	F#/Gb	G	G#/Ab	A
D#/Eb	E	F	F#/Gb	G	G#/Ab	A	A#/Bb
E	F	F#/Gb	G	G#/Ab	A	A#/Bb	B
F	F#/Gb	G	G#/Ab	A	A#/Bb	B	C
F#/Gb	G	G#/Ab	A	A#/Bb	B	C	C#/Db
G	G#/Ab	A	A#/Bb	B	C	C#/Db	D
G#/Ab	A	A#/Bb	B	C	C#/Db	D	D#/Eb
A	A#/Bb	B	C	C#/Db	D	D#/Eb	E
A#/Bb	B	C	C#/Db	D	D#/Eb	E	F
B	C	C#/Db	D	D#/Eb	E	F	F#/Gb

Song Screening Worksheet

As you pour through songbooks, hymnals and other collections seeking song candidates for your playlists, begin keeping a record of your findings so you don't have to start from scratch every week. Photocopy this sheet and fill in the blanks below. When you're finished, file it away! Don't toss it out! Note the examples: The bottom two rows are filled in to show how you might list songs about God's holiness.

Songs about: _____

On the above line, list the song content theme you are seeking, then list candidates you locate on the lines below.

Songs Title	Key	Time Signature	Tempo Family	Direction of Focus	Source
Examples: **Holy Holy Holy - Dykes**	**D**	**4/4**	**Family 1 76 bpm**	**Sung to God**	**Blue church hymnal**
Holy Holy Holy - Oliver	**E♭**	**4/4**	**Family 3 108 bpm**	**Sung to people**	**Best Praise Chorus Book**

WORSHIP PLAYLIST

Here are the songs, ordered and arranged, for our upcoming service.

Performance Date: _____

Song title:	Atmosphere/feel/attitude	Special notes:
Song section:	Singers notes:	Players notes:
Verse 1: Holy, Holy, Holy	Allison (soprano) only (softly)	Keys only, electric piano
Verse 2: Holy, Holy, Holy, all the . . .	Add Bob & ask congregation to sing	Add bass, soft drums with cross stick
Verse 3: Holy, Holy, Holy, through the . . .	All sing (med loud)	Add guitars, drums to play snare and rolls
Watch your music for the key change into verse 4!		
Verse 4: Holy, Holy, Holy, Lord God . . .	All sing (Louder, more poweful)	Add guitar distortion

Song title:	Atmosphere/feel/attitude	Special notes:
Song section:	Singers notes:	Players notes:

Sample

A document like this can bring together all of your planning and easily present it to your team at rehearsal. With this layout, you can fit two songs per page. Make as many copies of the blank playlist sheets as you need, fill in the details, and photocopy for your team members.

Use additional pages as necessary.

WORSHIP PLAYLIST

Here are the songs, ordered and arranged, for our upcoming service.

Performance Date: _____

Song title:	Atmosphere/feel/attitude	Special notes:
Song section:	Singers notes:	Players notes:

Song title:	Atmosphere/feel/attitude	Special notes:
Song section:	Singers notes:	Players notes:

Use additional pages as necessary.

PReReheaRSaL CheckLISt

Once you've chosen your playlist, use this helpful planning resource to get ready for rehearsal.

Rehearsal Date:_____ Performance Date:_____

Done☐ **Step 1: Pray for your ministry and your worship team members.**

Done☐ **Step 2: Get the music ready and in player's and singer's folders.**

Done☐ **Step 3: Choose the tempo for each song.**
> *Play excerpts from all songs back to back to check tempo compatibility.*

Done☐ **Step 4: Choose the instrumental and vocal arrangements for each song.**
> *Who plays and who sings on each verse?*

Done☐ **Step 5: Choose the intro measures.**
> *How will you start each song? When do the singers come in?*

Done☐ **Step 6: Play and talk through the transitions and modulations.**
> *What will you do between verses? Between songs? Between key changes?*
> *Using any codas? Are you talking between songs? Did you practice what you are going to say?*

Done☐ **Step 7: Review and mark tricky timing.**
> *Where are your singers and players likely to stumble?*
> *Make sure you can play/sing it correctly for teaching purposes.*

Done☐ **Step 8: Identify any lyrics needing special pronunciation.**
> *Are there any lyrics likely to be mispronounced? Underpronounced?*
> *Are there any long notes where the melody changes while holding?*

Done☐ **Step 9: Practice the non-melody parts.**
> *Can you play or sing the alto, tenor, and bass parts?*

Done☐ **Step 10: Plan the dynamics for your playlist.**
> *Where will the music change volume and/or tempo?*

Done☐ **Step 11: Play and sing through the entire playlist.**
> *Final check. How much time will the entire set require?_____*

Done☐ **Step 12: Prepare rehearsal order and playlist for your worship team.**
> *Use the reproducible playlist on page 147.*

Other Items:

Do you want to choose a brief teaching or instructional segment?

Your point: _____

_____

Time required to prepare for this rehearsal.

ReHearSaL PLanNeR

Fill in the blanks below and carry this sheet with you to rehearsal as your own private set of instructions.

Pray

Music education moment (if any) _____

Goals for the service _____

Discuss your goals for the upcoming service and any special events or unusual circumstances surrounding it.

Distribute the playlist

Quickly talk through each song and note any unique arrangements such as solos, non-typical styles.

Rehearsal order

*Get a base hit. Begin with the **easiest** song on the playlist.*

☐ Talk through or explain the arrangement in greater detail.
☐ Explain the roles of the singers and players (who sings/plays what and when).
☐ Explain repeats, dal segnos, codas, transitions.
☐ Explain the way you want the dynamics, feel, and flow of the song.
☐ Proactively warn of tricky places in the music where the team might stumble.
☐ After the song, pour on the affirmation when the team gets it right!

1st song to rehearse _____
2nd song to rehearse _____
3rd song to rehearse _____
4th song to rehearse _____
5th song to rehearse _____
6th song to rehearse _____
7th song to rehearse _____

Take a quick break!

Run the transitions between each song

Pick up from the last two lines of one song and play/sing through the first two lines of the following song.

Run the entire playlist

This time, top to bottom without stopping (unless there is a major train wreck).

Thank everyone and dismiss!

Sound Check

This quick and efficient sound check should precede every performance.
Help the team quickly get up, get done, and get off the platform.

Step 1. House speakers down/off. Monitors up.
Ask everyone to please be quiet unless checking their sound.

Step 2. Test individual singers at their mics in monitors only.
Ask each singer "Can you hear yourself in the monitor?"

Step 3. Balance all singers singing at once in monitors only.
Ask singers "Can each hear themselves when all are singing?"

Step 4. Test individual instrument players in monitors only.
Ask each player "Can you hear your instrument in the monitor?"

Step 5. Balance all players playing at once in monitors only.
Ask all players "Can you hear yourself when all instruments are playing?"

Step 6. Balance all singers and players in monitors only.
Ask all "Can you hear yourself in the monitor when everyone is playing and singing?"

Step 7. Bring up volume in house speakers.

THE HEART OF THE ARTIST

*A Character-Building Guide
for You and Your Ministry Team*

RORY NOLAND

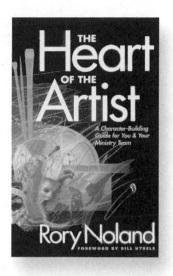

Find wisdom and encouragement that can help you survive the challenges and reap the rich joys of a ministry in the arts.

Written for artists by an artist, this frank, knowledge-able book deals head-on with issues every person in an arts ministry faces. With passion and conviction that come from personal experience, Rory Noland, music director for Willow Creek Community Church, addresses topics such as:

- Servanthood versus Stardom
- The Artist in Community
- Excellence versus Perfectionism
- Jealousy and Envy
- Managing Your Emotions
- The Spiritual Disciplines of the Artist

Between pride and self-abasement lies true humility—just one aspect of the balanced character God wants to instill in you as an actor, a musician, a visual artist, or other creative person involved in ministry. He's interested in your art *and* your heart.

Softcover: 0-310-22471-3

Pick up a copy today at your favorite bookstore!

WILLOW CREEK ASSOCIATION®

ZONDERVAN™

GRAND RAPIDS, MICHIGAN 49530

WWW.ZONDERVAN.COM

WORSHIP EVANGELISM

Inviting Unbelievers into the Presence of God

SALLY MORGENTHALER

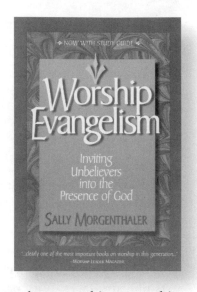

In *Worship Evangelism*, Sally Morgenthaler calls the church to consider the remarkable, untapped potential of worship as an opportunity of those who aren't yet followers of Jesus Christ as well as those who are to encounter the presence of God. Combining the best of traditional and contemporary worship music and practices, Morgenthaler shows how to achieve worship that's both culturally relevant and authentic. She helps pastors, worship leaders, and musicians

- Understand worship and its attraction for non-Christians
- Tear down walls that keep unbelievers from meeting God in church worship
- Make worship evangelism happen—in any culture

Morgenthaler draws on sound research and her extensive experience as a worship leader to offer an energetic, hands-on approach.

Now with a study guide that encourages group discussion and personal action, this timely book offers fresh vision for worship evangelism and provides the strategies to implement it.

Softcover: 0-310-22649-X   *www.pm4j.com*

Pick up a copy today at your favorite bookstore!

ZONDERVAN™

GRAND RAPIDS, MICHIGAN 49530

WWW.ZONDERVAN.COM

More Ready Than You Realize

Evangelism as Dance in the Postmodern Matrix

Brian D. McLaren

The words *evangelizing* and *postmoderns* and *matrix* are all buzzwords and are heard in the same sentence quite a bit these days. Now that evangelicals are alerted to the presence of change in our culture and discovering ways to adjust to that change, the next step is to take initiative and meet the new society head-on. We are talking about emerging-culture evangelism.

Brian McLaren is particularly gifted to show us how it can be done. His ministry at Cedar Ridge Community Church has an evangelistic emphasis and is growing. He is practicing what he preaches.

This book draws on his experiences and in a striking way. To those other three words we could add the word *Internet.* Or *email.* The context for this book is a series of real email conversations between Brian and a cyberseeker. Brian uses these conversations to elicit insights into the changing nature of evangelism in these postmodern times. In fact, he shows why the most profound synonym for the word *evangelism* is the term *disciple making.*

There are two appendices that can be used one-on-one or in small groups. One offers a Bible study on disciple making, the other a Scripture guide to some important concepts. These resources are effective with postmoderns because they take the approach that preachers are using more and more—the principle of "try it for a while and see if it works."

The range of readers for this book includes college students in parachurch groups (such as InterVarsity or Campus Crusade), but it's really as wide as the Internet. Moreover, while the book is effective for individuals, it also appeals to church small groups, not to mention the pastors and church leaders themselves.

This is a book for doing evangelism a.k.a. disciple making. Not a tell-me book, but a show-me book.

Softcover: 0-310-23964-8

www.crcc.org
www.emergentvillage.org

WORSHIP OLD AND NEW

ROBERT E. WEBER

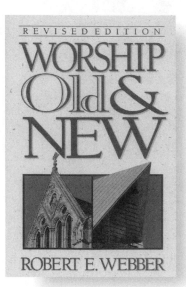

In the first edition of *Worship Old and New*, Robert E. Webber introduced an approach to worship that blended historical and traditional practices with contemporary elements. Since then, the spreading fires of worship renewal have provided opportunity for fresh consideration. This significantly revised edition is the result of Webber's interaction with current worship trends. It is intended to be used both in the classroom and by those who want to improve worship in the local church. Now reformatted for an easier, logical approach to worship theology, *Worship Old and New* is divided into four major sections, addressing the biblical foundation of worship, its theology, its history, and its practice. New information has been incorporated into each section to give the reader a better grasp of the biblical themes of worship, a deeper understanding of Old Testament customs, and a solid grounding in twentieth-century renewal movements. Especially significant is a re-examination of the actual practice of worship that goes beyond the merely academic to provide a practical perspective through the eyes of the worship leader and those who worship. Well-versed in the best of both past and present, *Worship Old and New,* is a scholarly, up-to-date, and thought-provoking resource for those serious about exploring worship.

Hardcover: 0-310-47990-8

Pick up a copy today at your favorite bookstore!

ZONDERVAN™

GRAND RAPIDS, MICHIGAN 49530

WWW.ZONDERVAN.COM

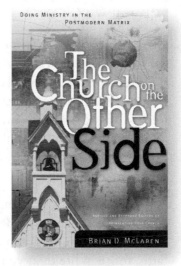

FINDING FAITH

A Self-Discovery Guide for Your Spiritual Quest

BRIAN D. MCLAREN

Real faith isn't blind believism. It is a process that engages your intellect as well as your emotions. If you think faith requires turning your back on truth and intellectual honesty, then this is one book you must read. It is fresh, thought-provoking, affirming, and challenging.

Finding Faith calls you neither to a blind leap in the dark nor to a cold rationalism that denies your deepest intuitions and spiritual longings. Rather, in the tradition of C. S. Lewis's *Mere Christianity* and M. Scott Peck's *The Road Less Traveled,* it summons you to reflection and honesty. With logic, passion, and an evenhandedness that the thinking person will appreciate, this book helps you face your obstacles to faith by focusing not on what to believe but on how to believe.

Whether you want to strengthen the faith you have, renew the faith you lost, or discover faith for the first time, *Finding Faith* can coach, inspire, encourage, and guide you. And it can help you discover, through a dynamic, authentic, and growing faith, more in life than you'd ever imagined or hoped for.

Hardcover: 0-310-22542-6
Softcover: 0-310-23838-2

www.crcc.org
www.emergentvillage.org

Pick up a copy today at your favorite bookstore!

ZONDERVAN™

GRAND RAPIDS, MICHIGAN 49530

WWW.ZONDERVAN.COM

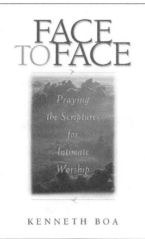

FACE TO FACE
Praying Scriptures for Intimate Worship

KENNETH BOA

Like many believers, you may wonder how to integrate heartfelt worship into your private devotional times. *Face to Face: Praying the Scriptures for Intimate Worship* helps you bridge the gap between Bible reading and intimate, joyous worship. Adapting and personalizing select passages from the Bible, Dr. Kenneth Boa guides you through three months of daily prayers of

- Adoration
- Renewal
- Intercession
- Thanksgiving
- Confession
- Petition
- Affirmation

Praying the Scriptures will help you to pray with greater assurance and satisfaction. You'll rediscover the Bible as a rich, personal wellspring of worship—worship that allows you to express to God all that's in your heart, even as he reveals the depths of his own heart to you.

In *Face to Face: Praying the Scriptures for Intimate Worship*, select Scripture verses become personal prayers of intimacy and adoration that allow you to express your heart more fully to God.

Softcover: 0-310-92550-9

We want to hear from you. Please send your comments about this book to us in care of the address below. Thank you.

GRAND RAPIDS, MICHIGAN 49530

WWW.ZONDERVAN.COM